Skills Link™

Everyday Mathematics®

Skills Link™

Everyday Mathematics®

Cumulative Practice Sets

A Division of The McGraw-Hill Companies

Columbus, Ohio
Chicago, Illinois

Photo Credits

Cover—Bill Burlingham/Photography
Photo Collage—Herman Adler Design

www.sra4kids.com

SRA/McGraw-Hill

*A Division of The **McGraw·Hill** Companies*

Send all inquiries to:
SRA/McGraw-Hill
P.O. Box 812960
Chicago, IL 60681

Printed in the United States of America.

ISBN 1-57039-937-9

10 11 12 13 14 15 VHG 09 08 07 06 05

Contents

Name Date

Practice Set 1

1. Write the number.

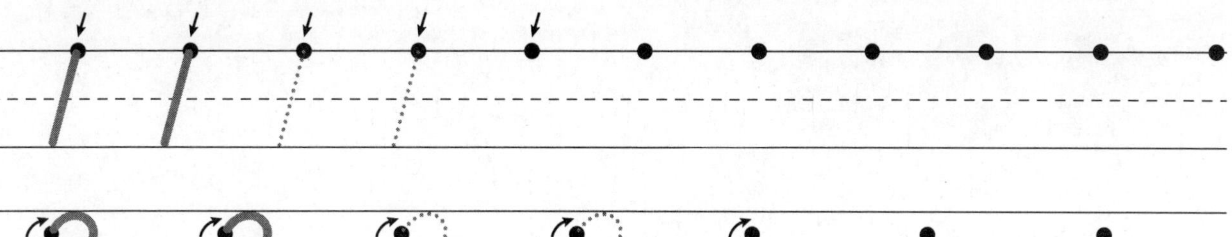

2. Draw a picture of 1 thing.

3. Draw a picture of 2 things.

4. Draw circles to show 5.

5. Draw sticks to show 10.

Name Date

Practice Set 2

1. Draw 1 more.

---

2. Show 1 less. Make an **X.**

---

3. Count by 1s. Connect the dots.

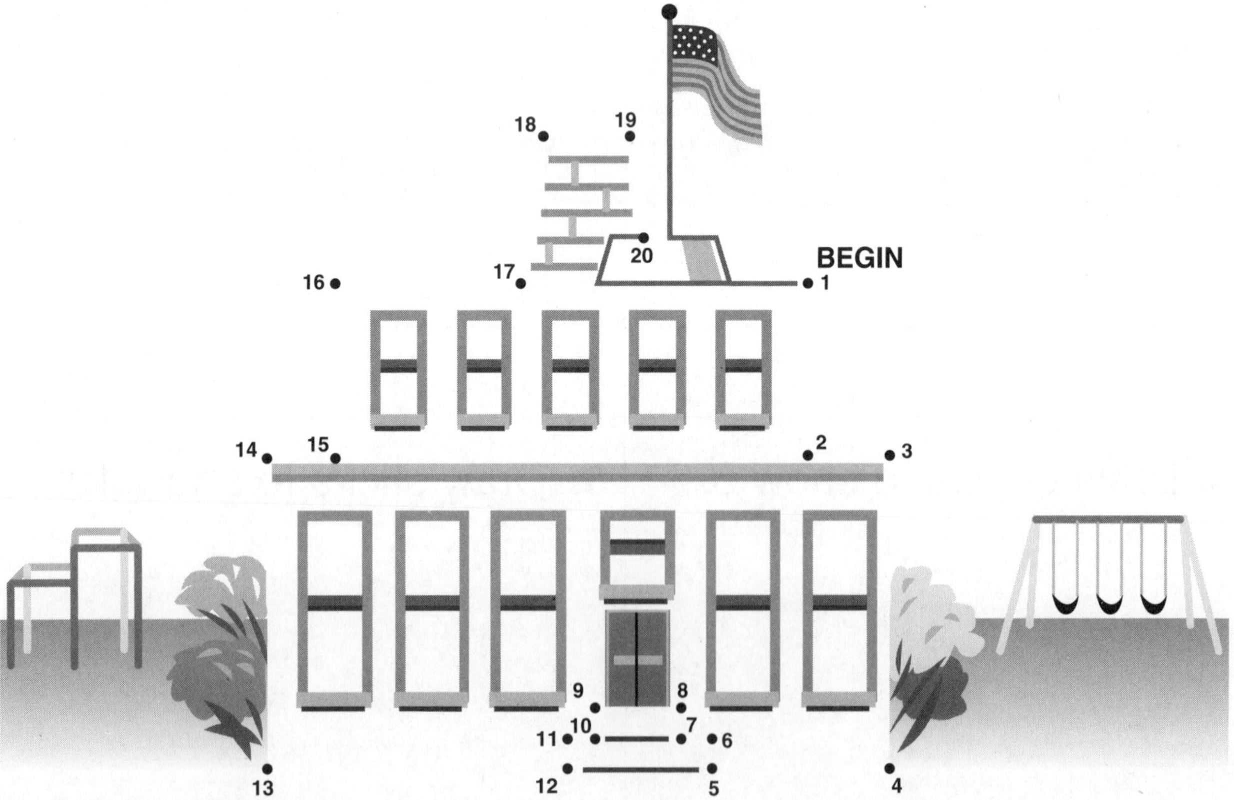

Use with or after Lesson 1.5.

Name Date

Practice Set 3

Circle the larger number in each pair.

1.

2.

Circle the mystery number below each number line.

3.

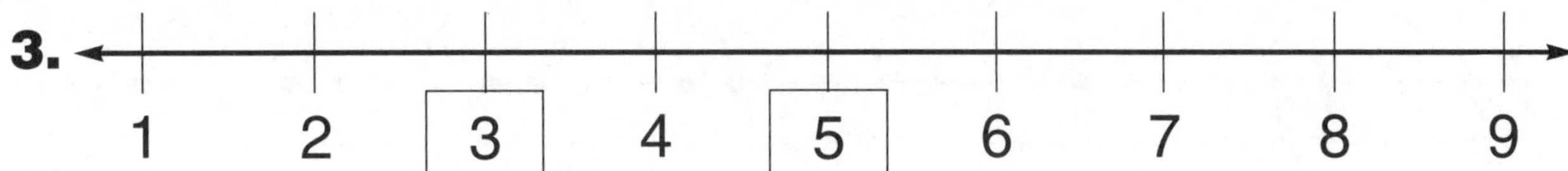

2 4 7

4.

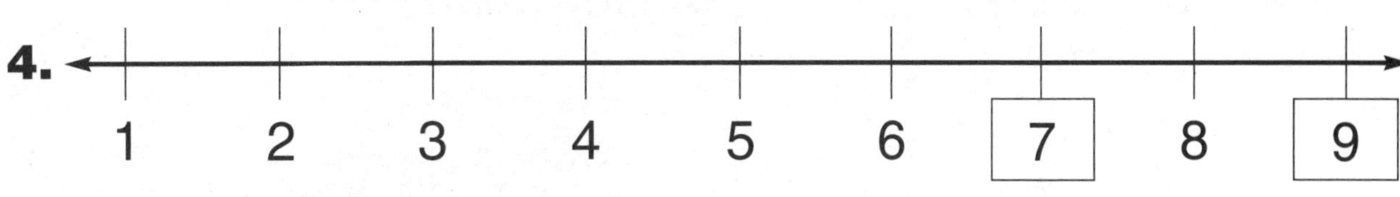

2 5 8

5. Circle the number that **could** be the mystery number.

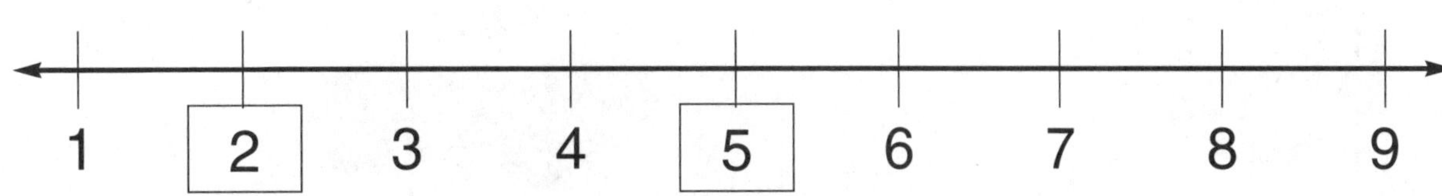

3 6 8

Name Date

Practice Set 4

Make tallies.

Example 7 𝍸 ||

1. 5 ______

2. 4 ______

3. 9 ______

4. 11 ______

5. 16 ______

6. Write the number.

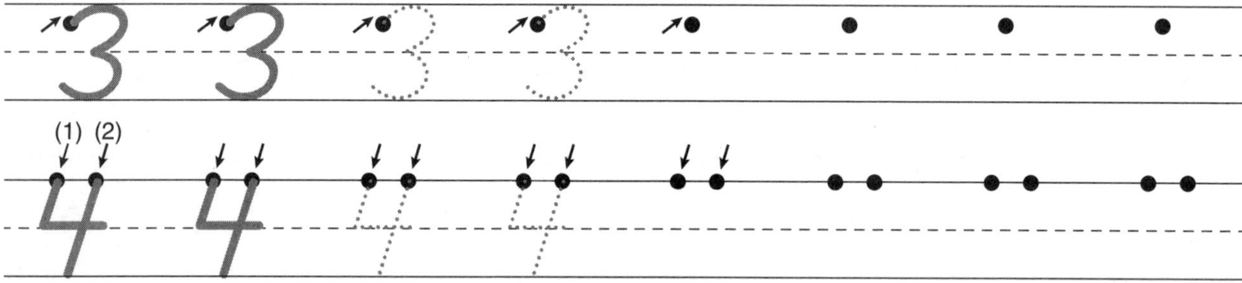

7. How many balls?

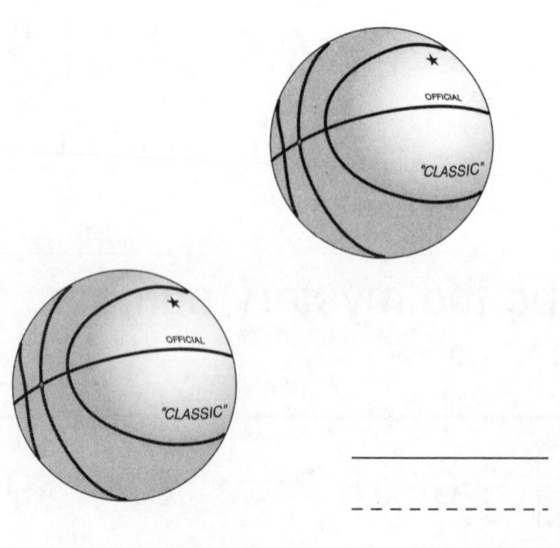

______

8. How many cars?

______

Use with or after Lesson 1.7.

Name Date

Practice Set 5

1. Fill in the missing numbers.
Then circle the 10 and the 15.
Then cross out the 7.

February

Sunday	Monday	Tuesday	Wednesday	Thursday	Friday	Saturday
1	____	____	____	____	____	7
8	9	10	11	12	13	14
15	16	17	18	19	20	21
22	23	24	25	26	27	28

2. Write the number.

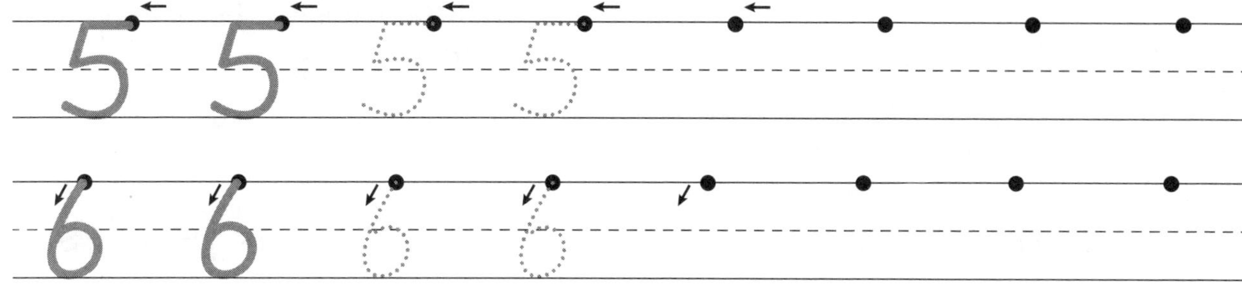

Name Date

Practice Set 6

Make the shape. Use your Pattern-Block Template.

1.

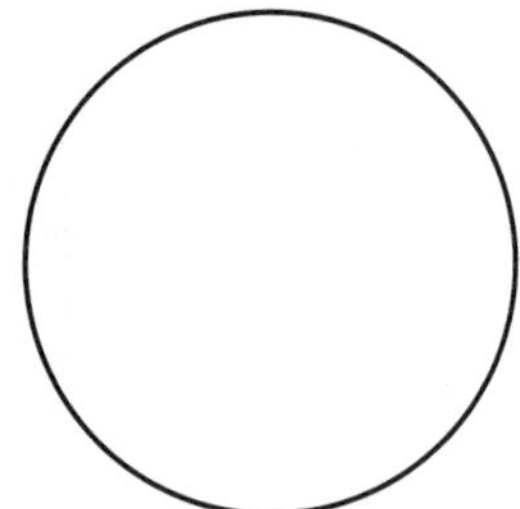

2.

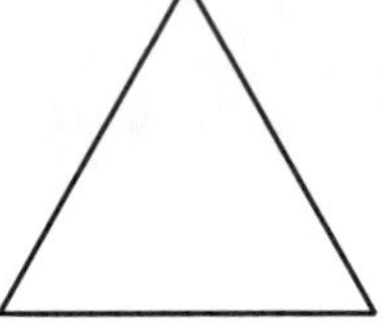

3.

4. You roll  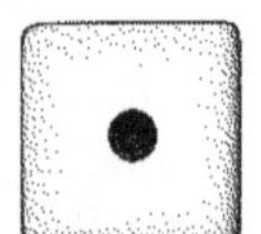.

Circle that many pennies.

5. You roll 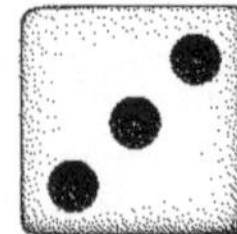 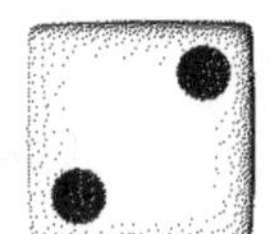.

Circle that many pennies.

Use with or after Lesson 1.11.

Name Date

Practice Set 7

Match each picture to a °F temperature.

1.

2.

3.

90
80
70
60
50
40
30
20

90
80
70
60
50
40
30
20

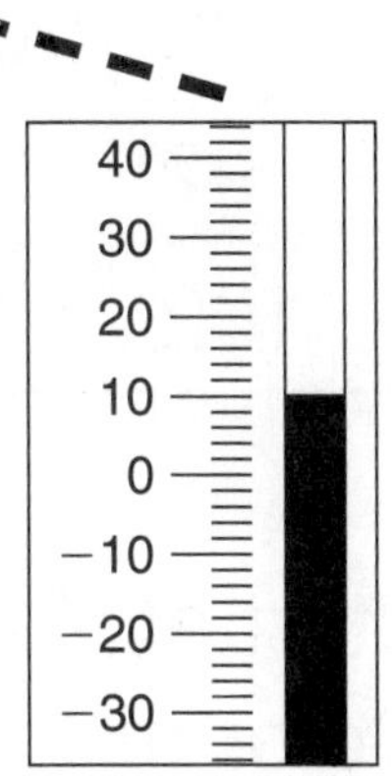

4. Show how old you are. Use tally marks. ____________

5. Show how many pencils you have.
Use tally marks. ____________

Circle the larger number.

6. 5 8

7. 21 36

Name Date

Practice Set 8

									0
1	2	3	4	5	6	7	8	9	10
11	12	13	14	15	16	17	18	19	20
21	22	23	24	25	26	27	28	29	30
31	32	33	34	35	36	37	38	39	40
41	42	43	44	45	46	47	48	49	50
51	52	53	54	55	56	57	58	59	60
61	62	63	64	65	66	67	68	69	70
71	72	73	74	75	76	77	78	79	80
81	82	83	84	85	86	87	88	89	90
91	92	93	94	95	96	97	98	99	100
101	102	103	104	105	106	107	108	109	110

1. Start at 7 and count up 8 spaces.
   Color the rectangle **red.**

2. Start at 45 and count up 9 spaces.
   Color the rectangle **yellow.**

3. Start at 18 and count back 7 spaces.
   Color the rectangle **purple.**

4. Start at 102 and count back 6 spaces.
   Color the rectangle **green.**

5. Start at 103 and count back 10 spaces.
   Color the rectangle **blue.**

Name Date

Practice Set 9

Circle each one that shows 10 pennies.

1.

2.

3.

4.

5.

6.

7. Write the number.

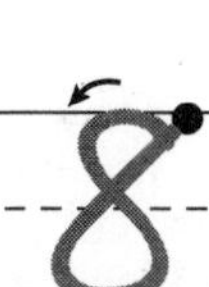

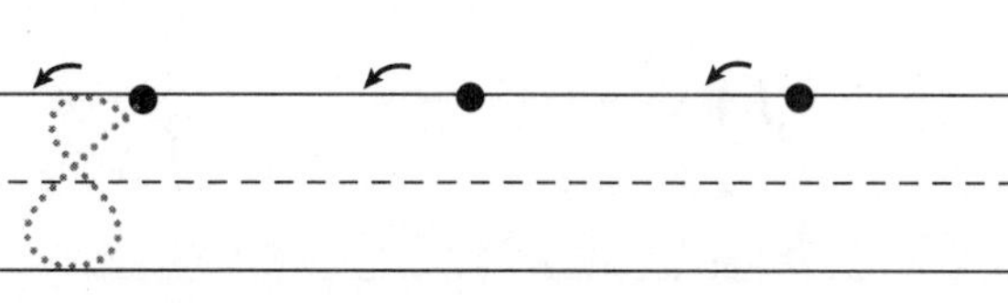

Name Date

Practice Set 10

1. Write the missing numbers.

2. Circle the correct time.

9 o'clock	between 9 o'clock and 10 o'clock	10 o'clock

3. Write the number.

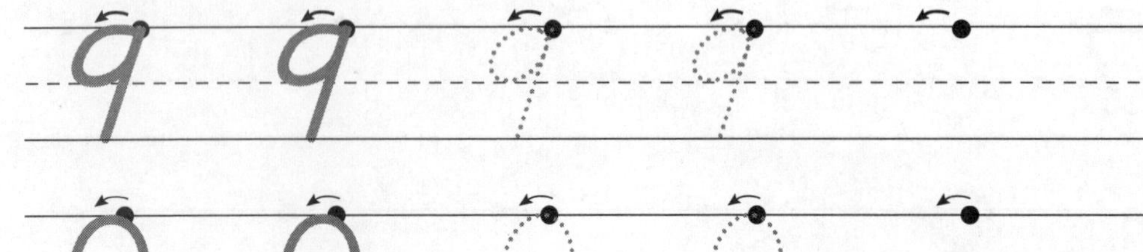

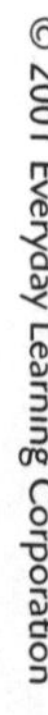

Use with or after Lesson 2.5.

Name Date

Practice Set 11

What time is it?

1.

_____ o'clock

2.

_____ o'clock

3.

_____ o'clock

Draw the hour hand.

4.

3 o'clock

5.

8 o'clock

6.

11 o'clock

7. Make a tally for 9.

8. Make a tally for 10.

9. Make a tally for 13.

10. Make a tally for 6.

Name Date

Practice Set 12

Match the dominoes.

1. 

2. 

3. 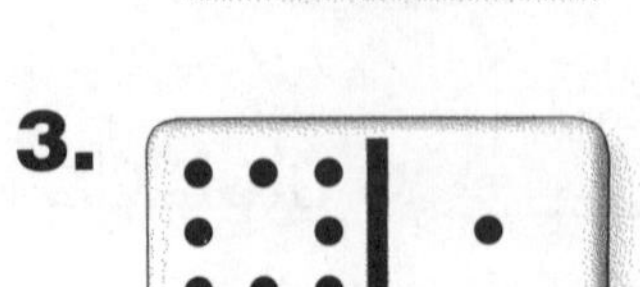

How many dots in all?

4. 

_____

5. 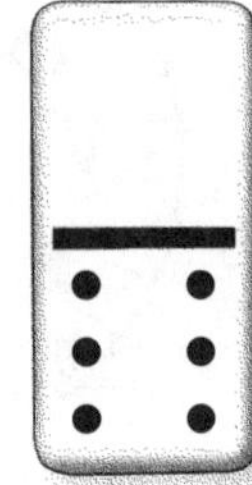

_____

Count by 1s.

Unit
cats

6. 4, 5, 6, ____, ____, ____, ____, ____

7. 16, 17, 18, ____, ____, ____, ____

8. 20, 21, 22, ____, ____, ____, ____

Use with or after Lesson 2.7.

Name Date

Practice Set 13

Draw Ⓝs and Ⓟs to show how much.

Example

1.        

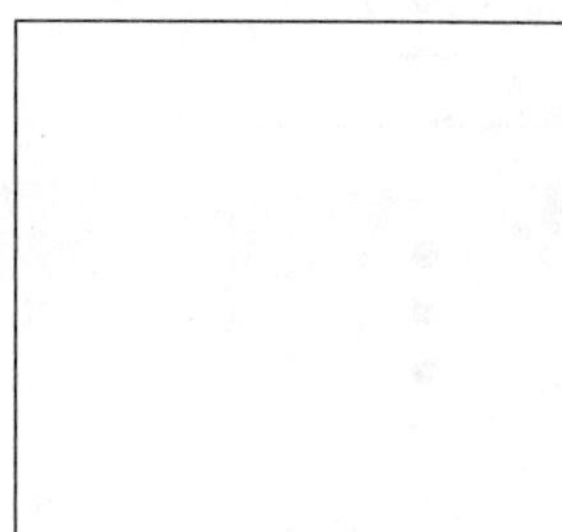

2.       

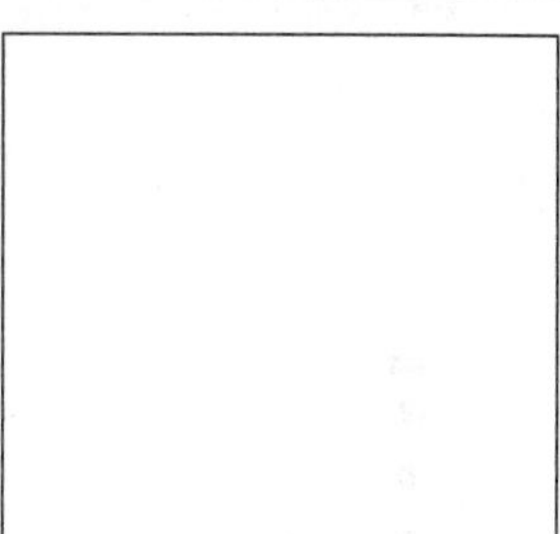

3. How many fingers? Count by 5s.

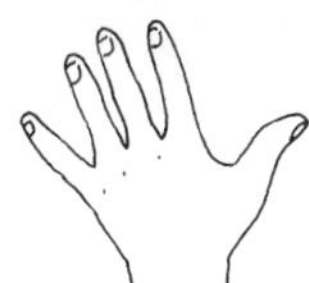 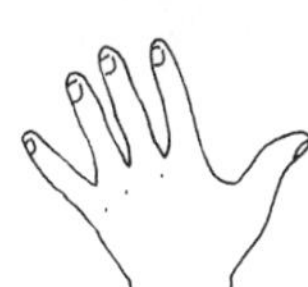 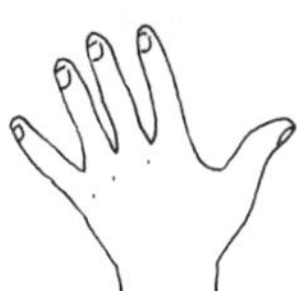 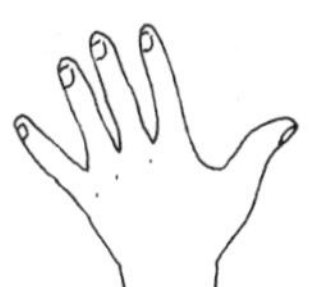 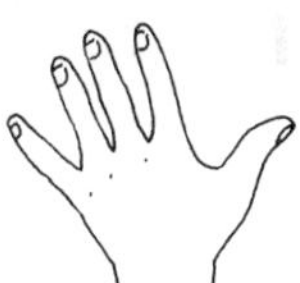

5, 10, ____, ____, ____, ____

4. Count by 5s.

40, ____, ____, 55, ____, ____, ____ ____, ____

Name Date

Practice Set 14

Count by 5s. Tell how much.

1.  

15 ¢

2.  

______ ¢

3.     

______ ¢

4.    

______ ¢

How much money?

5.       

______¢

6.    

______¢

Circle the larger number.

7. 11 12

8. 7 15

Use with or after Lesson 2.10.

Name Date

Practice Set 15

1. Cross out 3 pennies. How much money is left?

_______¢

2. Cross out 2 nickels. How much money is left?

_______¢

Draw Ⓝs and Ⓟs to show how much.

3. 7 cents

4. 12 cents

What time is it?

5.

_______:_______

6.

_______:_______

Name Date

Practice Set 16

Circle pairs. Then circle *even* or *odd*.

1.   

even **odd**

---

2.    

even **odd**

Draw the next shape.
Use your Pattern Block-Template.

3.  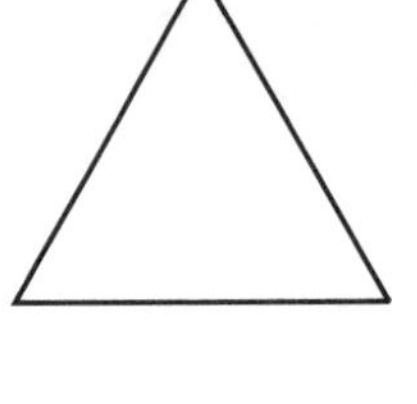 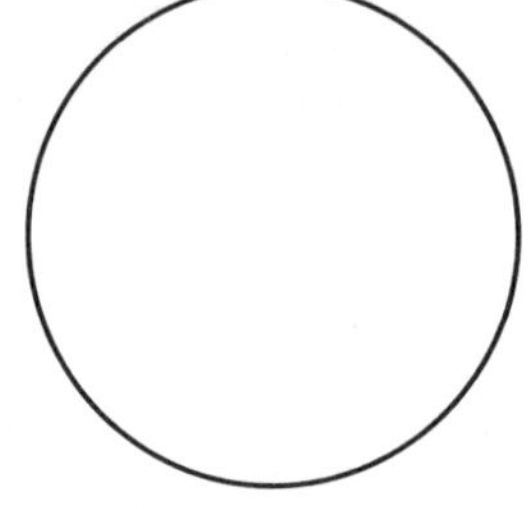 ______

4. 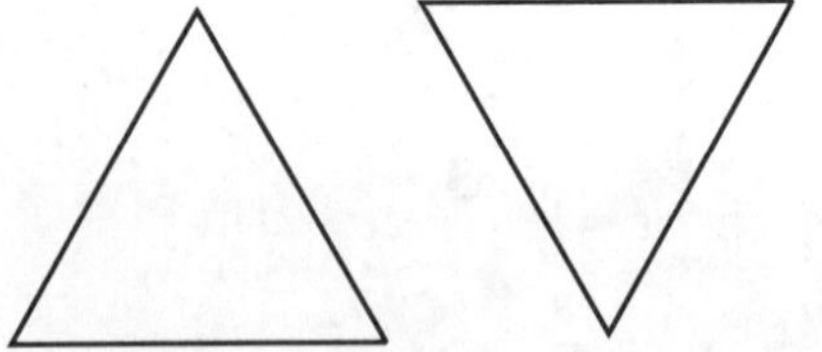 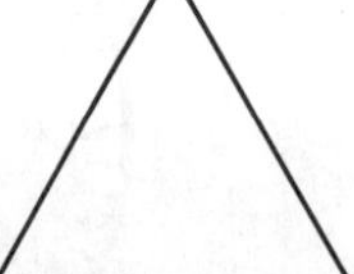 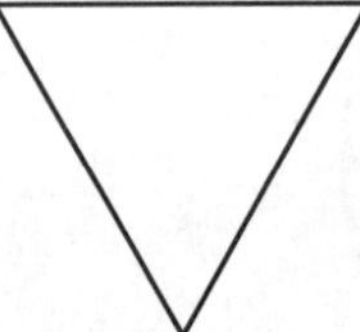 ______

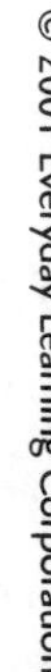

---

5. Count by 2s.

2, 4, 6, ____, ____, ____, ____, ____

Use with or after Lesson 3.2.

Name Date

Practice Set 17

1. Count by 3s. Put an **X** over each number you count.

									0
1	2	3	4	5	6	7	8	9	10
11	12	13	14	15	16	17	18	19	20
21	22	23	24	25	26	27	28	29	30
31	32	33	34	35	36	37	38	39	40
41	42	43	44	45	46	47	48	49	50
51	52	53	54	55	56	57	58	59	60
61	62	63	64	65	66	67	68	69	70
71	72	73	74	75	76	77	78	79	80
81	82	83	84	85	86	87	88	89	90
91	92	93	94	95	96	97	98	99	100
101	102	103	104	105	106	107	108	109	110

Write the missing numbers.

2. 8 ___ ___ 11 ___ ___ ___

3. ___ 22 ___ ___ ___ 26 ___

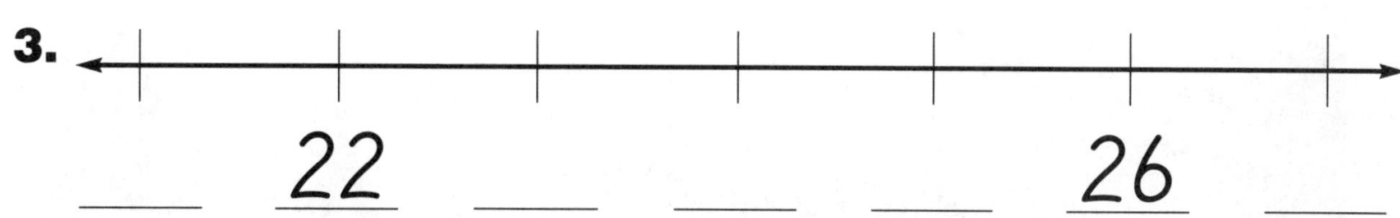

Name Date

Practice Set 18 

How many dots? Write *odd* or *even.*

1. ______ ____________

2. ______ ____________

3. ______ ____________

4. 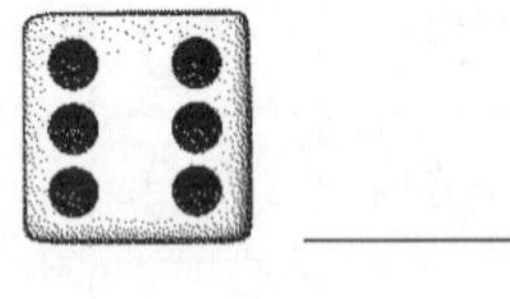 ______ ____________

5. 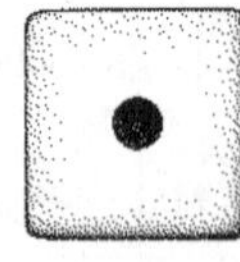 ______ ____________

6. 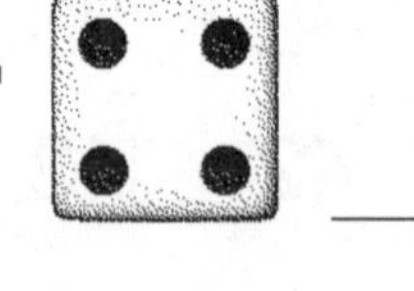 ______ ____________

Count by 10s. Connect the dots.

7.

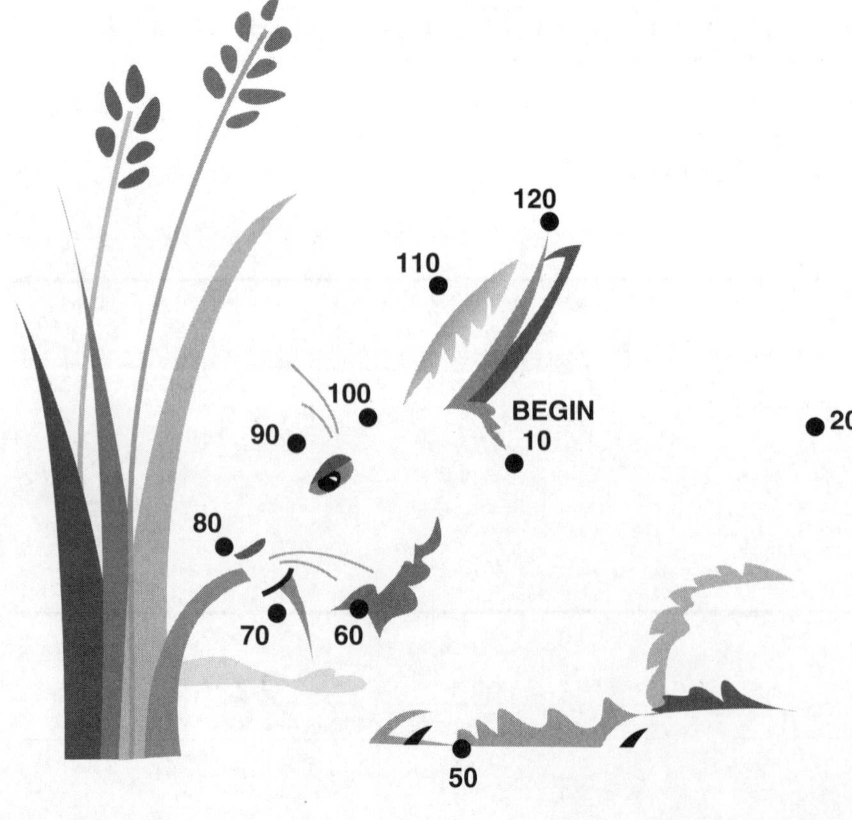

Name Date

Practice Set 19

1. Count by 2s. Show your counts.

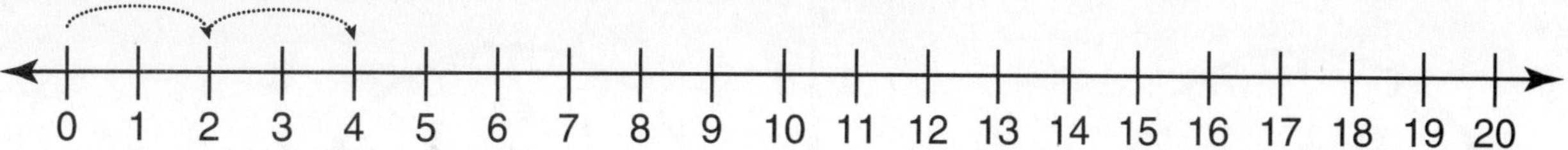

2. Count back by 1s. Show your counts.

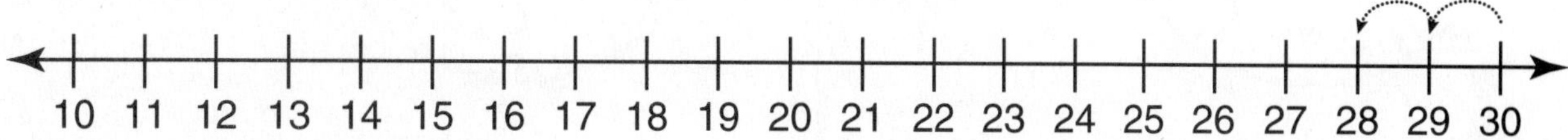

Record the time.

3.

about ____ o'clock

4.

between ____:00 and ____:00

5.

about ____:00

6.

just after ____ o'clock

Name Date

Practice Set 20

What time is it?

1.

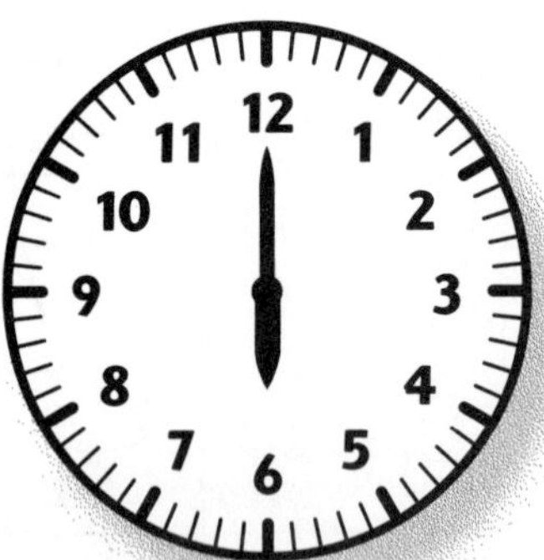

______ o'clock

2.

______ o'clock

3.

half-past ______ o'clock

4.

half-past ______ o'clock

How much money?

5.       

\$0.____ or ____¢

6. 

\$0.____ or ____¢

7.        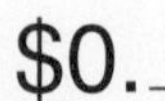

\$0.____ or ____¢

Name Date

Practice Set 21

Fill in the frames.

Example

Rule
Count by 2s

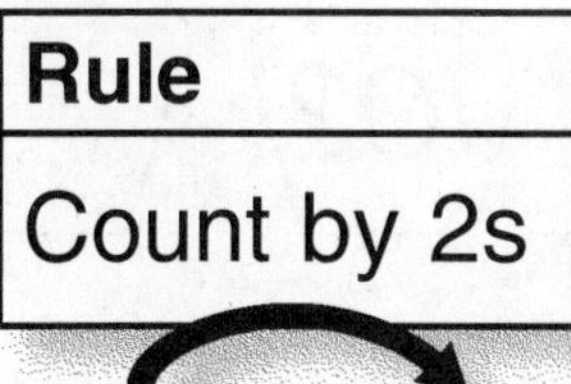

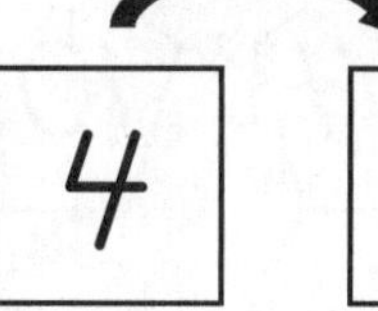

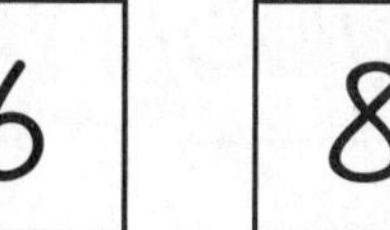

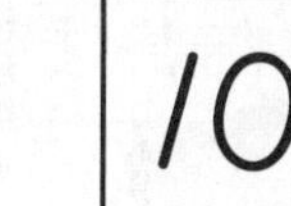

4 6 8 10 12

1.

Rule
Count by 5s

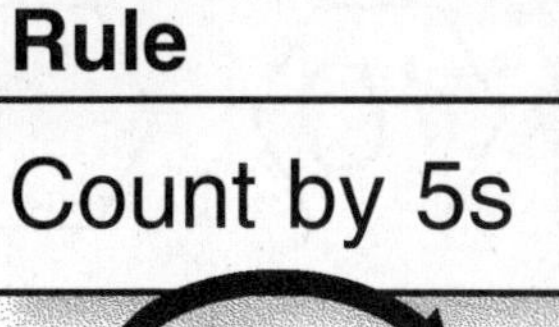

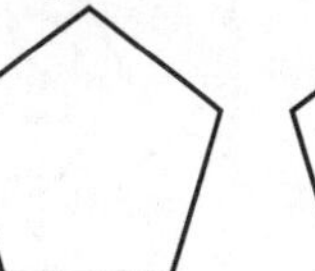

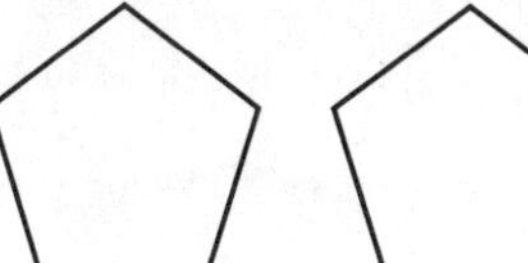

10 15

2.

Rule
Count by 2s

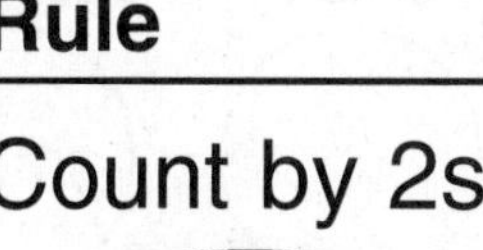

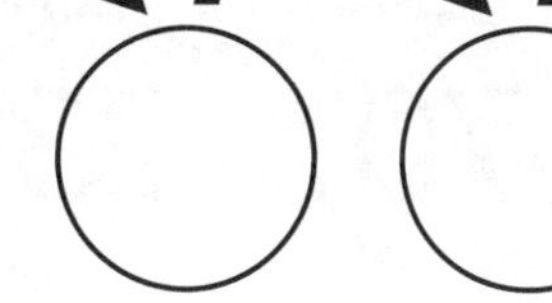

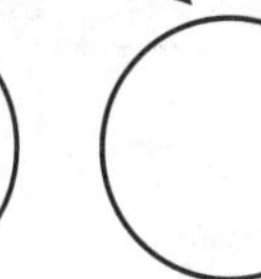

14

Tell the time.

3.

_______ o'clock

4.

half-past _______ o'clock

Name Date

Practice Set 22

Fill in the rule box. Complete the frames.

1\.

104

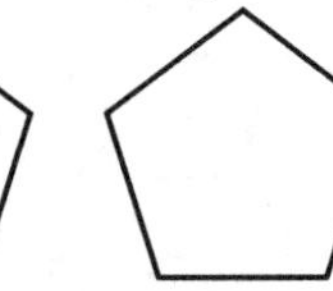

2\.

3\.

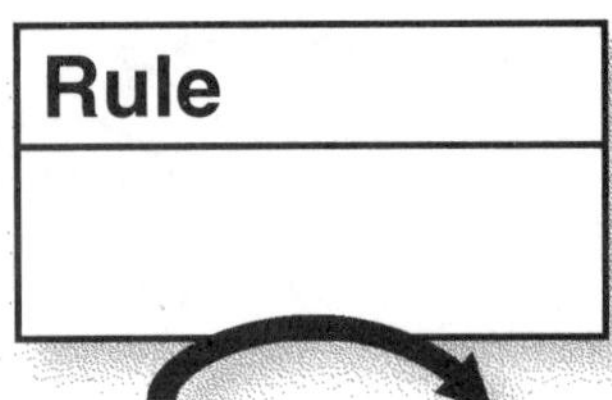

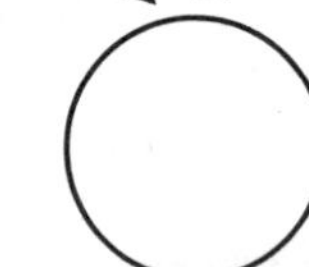

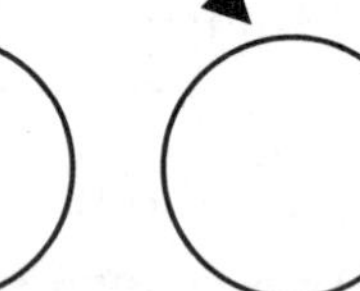

Tell the time.

4\.

half-past ______ o'clock

5\.

half-past ______ o'clock

Use with or after Lesson 3.9.

Name Date

Practice Set 23

1. Use your calculator. Count up by 2s.

Press (ON/C) (2) (+) (2) (=) (=) (=) (=)

2, 4, 6, 8, ___, ___, ___, ___, ___,

20, ___, ___, ___, ___, ___, ___, ___, 36

2. Use your calculator. Count back by 2s.

Press (ON/C) (3) (4) (−) (2) (=) (=) (=) (=)

34, 32, 30, 28, ___, ___, ___, ___, ___,

16, ___, ___, ___, ___, ___, ___, ___, ___

Fill in the rule box. Complete the frames.

3.

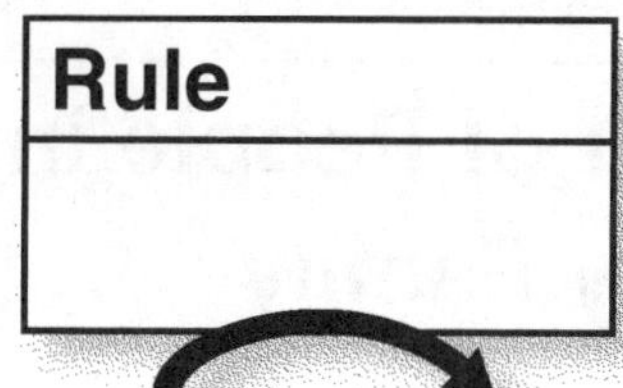

4.

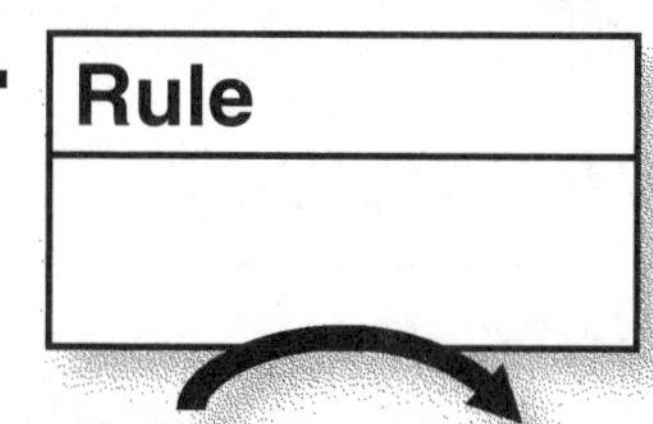

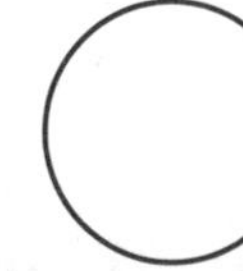

Name Date

Practice Set 24

How much money?

1. 1  = ____ 

2. 20  = ____ 

3. 2  = ____ 

4. 2  = ____ 

5.      $0.____ or ____¢

6.     $0.____ or ____¢

7.       $0.____ or ____¢

Answer each question.

How many children have . . .

8. 5 people in their family?

____ children

9. 4 people in their family?

____ children

10. 2 or 3 people in their family?

____ children

Number of People in My Family	
2	///
3	~~////~~
4	~~////~~ ~~////~~ ~~////~~ /
5	~~////~~ ~~////~~ //
6	//

Use with or after Lesson 3.12.

Name Date

Practice Set 25

Write 3 numbers for each domino.

1.

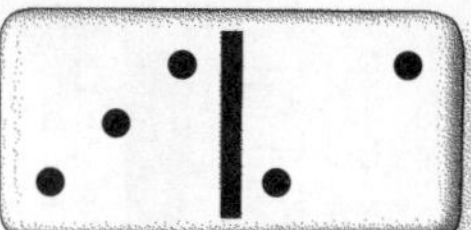

Total	
Part	Part
3	2

2.

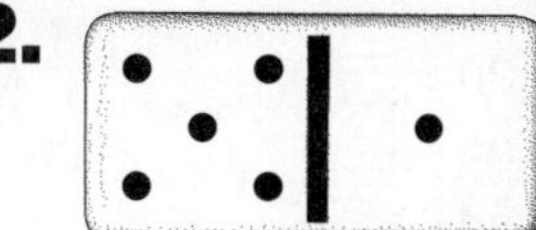

Total	
Part	Part

3.

Total	
Part	Part

4.

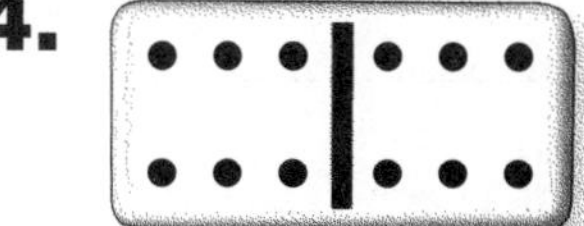

Total	
Part	Part

5.

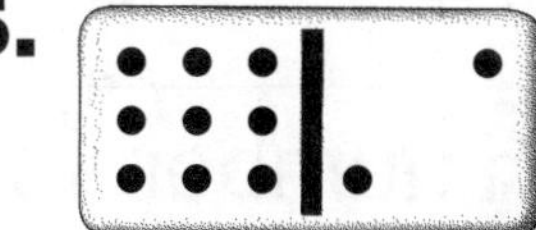

Total	
Part	Part

6.

Total	
Part	Part

Write the numbers before and after.

7. ____, 38, ____

8. ____, 92, ____

9. ____, 79, ____

10. ____, 100, ____

Practice Set 26

Write the °F temperature.

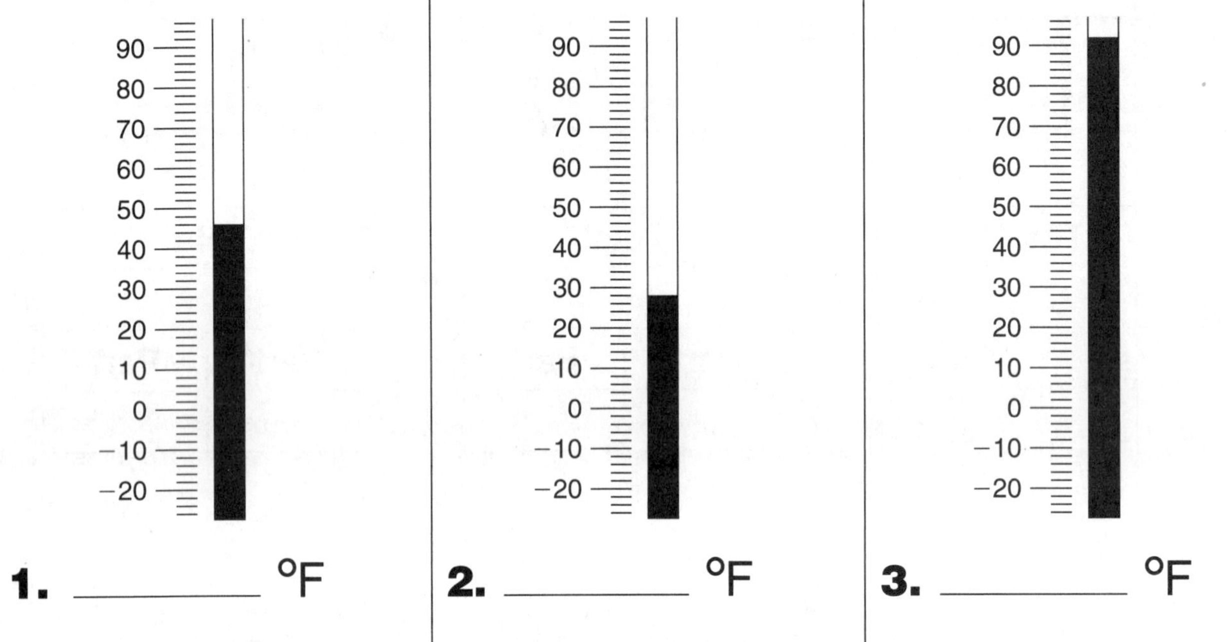

1. _______ °F **2.** _______ °F **3.** _______ °F

4. Count by 3s. Write each number you count.

									0
1	2	3	4	5	6	7	8	9	10
11		13	14		16	17		19	20
	22	23		25	26		28	29	
31	32		34	35		37	38		40
41		43	44		46	47		49	50
	52	53		55	56		58	59	
61	62		64	65		67	68		70
71		73	74		76	77		79	80
	82	83		85	86		88	89	
91	92		94	95		97	98		100
101		103	104		106	107		109	110

Use with or after Lesson 4.1.

Name Date

Practice Set 27

About how long?

1. 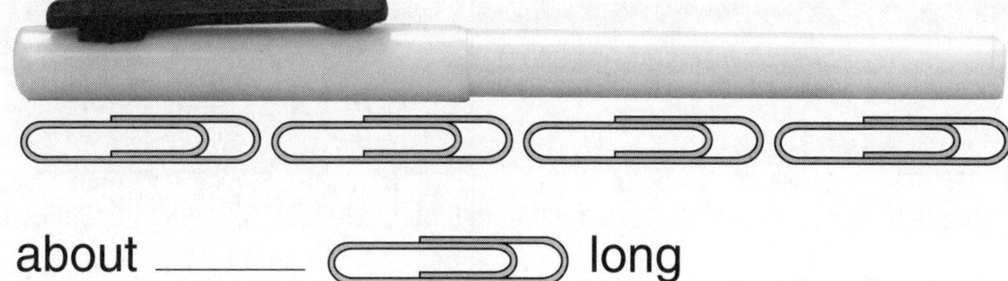

about ______ [paper clip] long

2.

about ______ [paper clip] long

3.

about ______ [paper clip] long

4. Count back.

17, 16, ______, ______, ______, ______, ______

Write the numbers before and after.

5. ______, 19, ______

6. ______, 43, ______

7. ______, 30, ______

8. ______, 27, ______

Name Date

Practice Set 28

Use a ruler. Measure.

1.

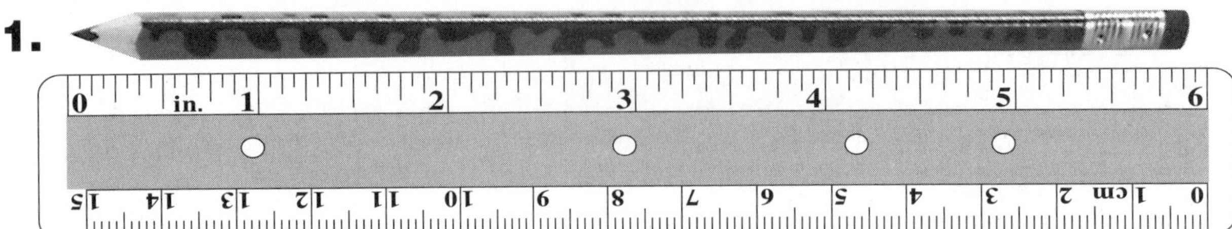

about ______ inches long

2.

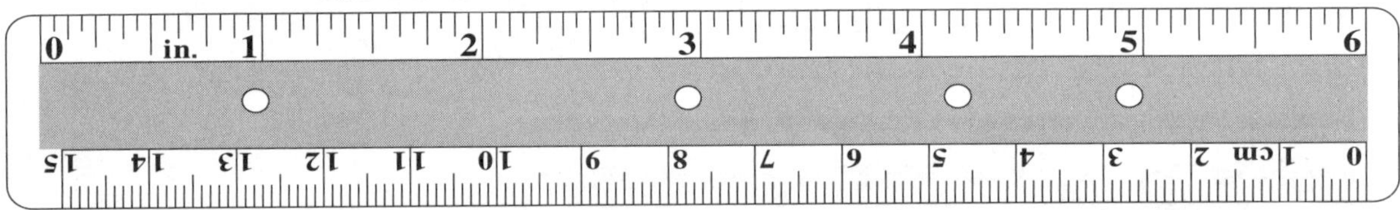

about ______ inches long

3.

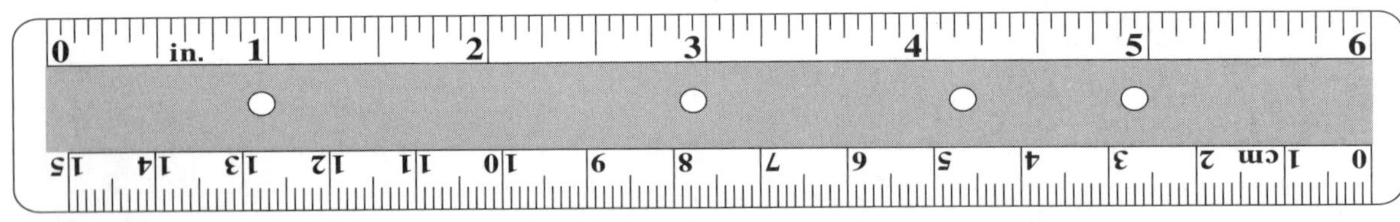

about ______ inches long

Count by 10s. Show your counts.

4.

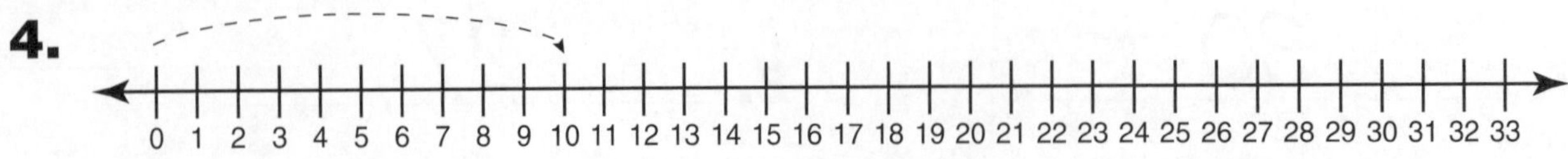

5.

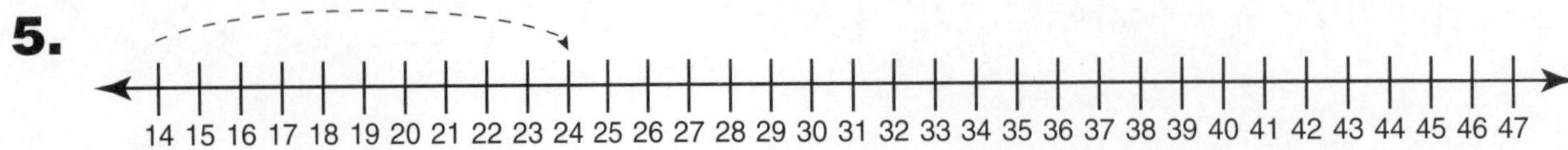

Use with or after Lesson 4.4.

Name Date

Practice Set 29

Children's Heights

Sally	Ken	Drew	Kendra	Lorna
41 in.	46 in.	46 in.	46 in.	49 in.

1. How tall is Sally?

Sally is ______ inches tall.

2. Who is the tallest?

______________________ is the tallest.

3. How many children are 46 inches tall?

______ children are 46 inches tall.

Write the numbers before and after.

4. ____, 17, ____

5. ____, 30, ____

Fill in the missing numbers. Count down.

6. 10, ____, ____, 7, ____, ____, ____, ____, ____, ____

7. 18, ____, 16, ____, ____, ____, ____, ____, ____, ____

8. 33, ____, ____, 30, ____, ____, ____, ____, ____, ____

Name Date

Practice Set 30

Record the time.

1.

_____ o'clock

2.

half-past _____ o'clock

3.

quarter-past _____ o'clock

4.

quarter-to _____ o'clock

Count by 10s.

Unit
dogs

5. 10, 20, _____, _____, _____, _____

6. 40, _____, 60, _____, _____, _____

7. 50, _____, _____, _____, 90, _____

Use with or after Lesson 4.8.

Name Date

Practice Set 31

									0
1	2	3	4	5	6	7	8	9	10
11	12	13	14	15	16		18	19	20
21		23	24	25	26		28	29	30
31		33	34	35	36		38	39	40
41		43	44	45	46		48	49	50
									60
61	62	63		65				69	70
71	72		74	75	76	77	78	79	
81	82	83	84		86		88	89	90
	92	93	94	95				99	100
		103	104			107	108	109	
	112	113			116	117		119	120

1. Fill in the missing numbers on the grid.
2. Start at 7. Count by 5s.
   Put an **X** over each number you count.
3. Find three odd numbers. Draw circles around them.

Fill in the missing numbers. Count down.

4. 75, ____, ____, 72, ____, ____, 69, ____, ____

5. 100, 99, ____, ____, ____, ____, ____, ____, ____

Name Date

Practice Set 32

Find the sum on each pair of dice.

Example

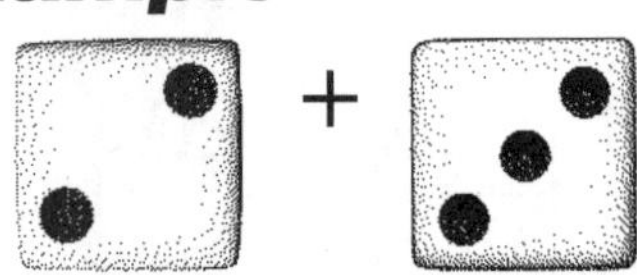

2 + 3 = 5

1.

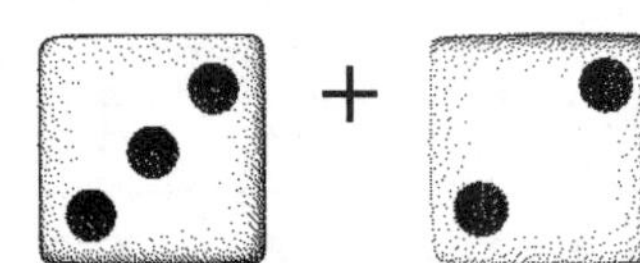

___ + ___ = ___

2.

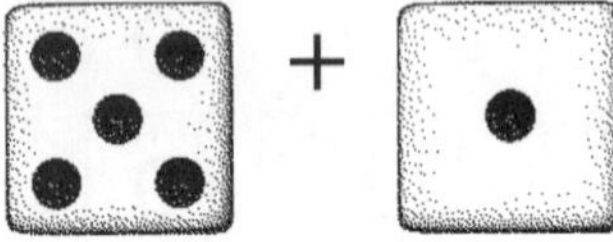

___ + ___ = ___

3.

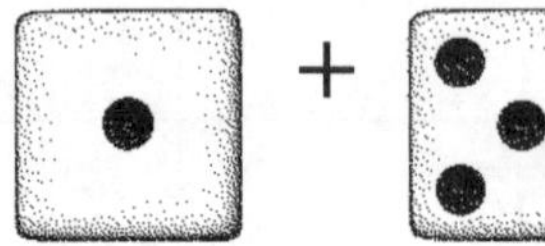

___ + ___ = ___

4.

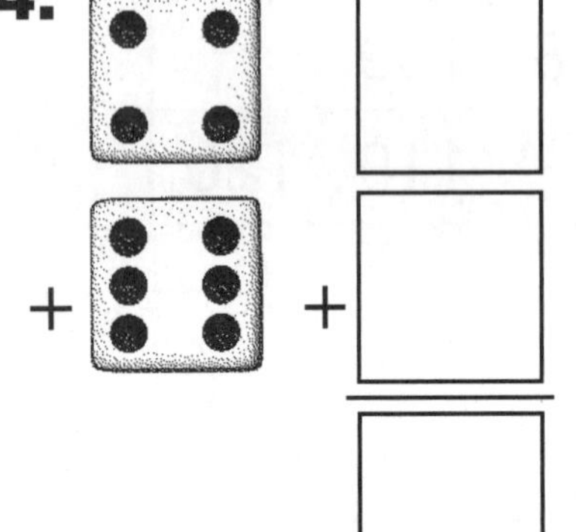

5.

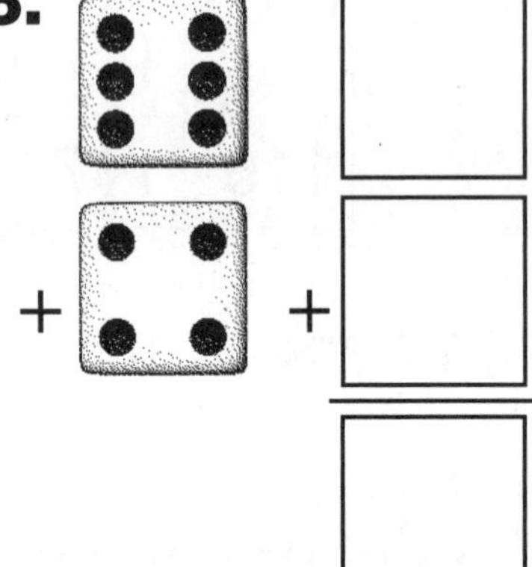

6.

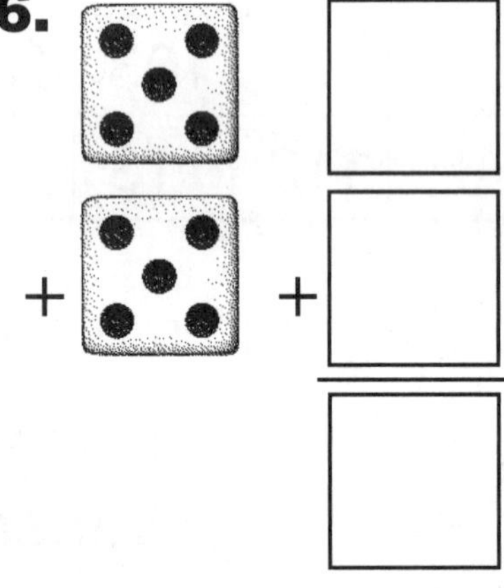

Write the missing numbers.

7.

-1 0 ___ ___ ___ ___ ___ 6

8.

8 ___ 10 ___ ___ ___ ___ ___

Use with or after Lesson 4.11.

Name Date

Practice Set 33

Find each sum. Then color.

Colors	
6	yellow
7	red
8	green
9	blue
10	orange

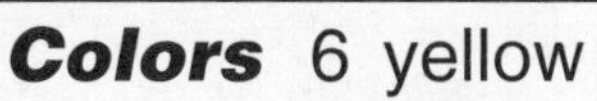

$2 + 6$

$1 + 6$

$5 + 4$

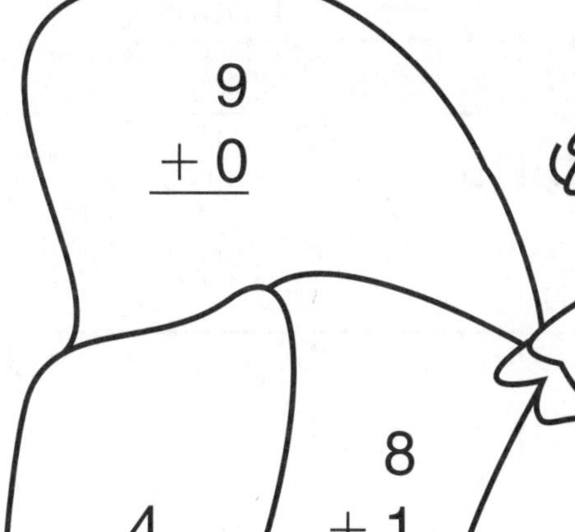

$9 + 0$

$8 + 1$

$4 + 4$

$4 + 5$

$2 + 7$

$5 + 2$

$\_\_\_\_ = 0 + 8$

$6 + 3 = \_\_\_\_$

$4 + 3$

$5 + 5$

$5 + 3$

$2 + 6 = \_\_\_\_$

$3 + 3 = \_\_\_\_$

$1 + 5 = \_\_\_\_$

$1 + 7$

Name Date

Practice Set 34

1. Use your calculator. Count up by 10s.

Press (ON/C) (1) (0) (+) (1) (0) (=) (=) (=)

10, 20, 30, 40, ____, ____, ____, ____, ____,

____, ____, ____, ____, ____, ____, ____, ____, ____,

____, ____, ____, ____, ____, ____, ____, ____, ____

Show how much using the fewest coins.

Draw Ⓠs, Ⓓs, Ⓝs, or Ⓟs.

2. $0.28 or 28¢

3. $0.41 or 41¢

4. Show 35 cents two different ways.

Name Date

Practice Set 35

Use <, >, or =.

< means *is less than*
> means *is greater than*
= means *is the same as*
= means *is equal to*

1. 12 ☐ 19

2. 43 ☐ 34

3. 115 ☐ 115

4. 58 ☐ 68

5. 124 ☐ 224

6. 300 ☐ 299

Unit
pounds

Mark the end of the line segment.

Example 3 inches

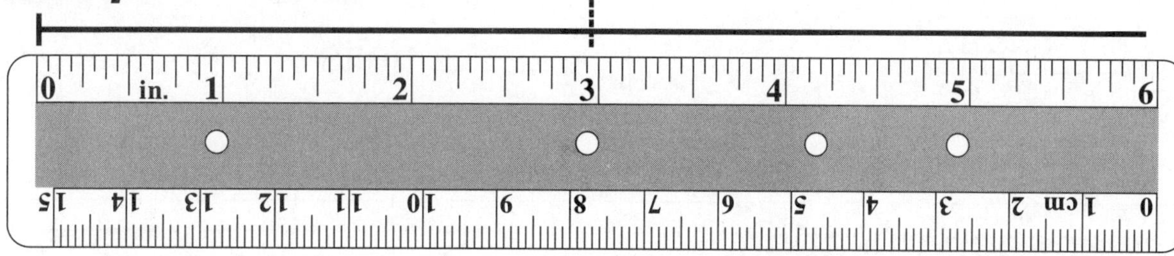

7. 5 inches

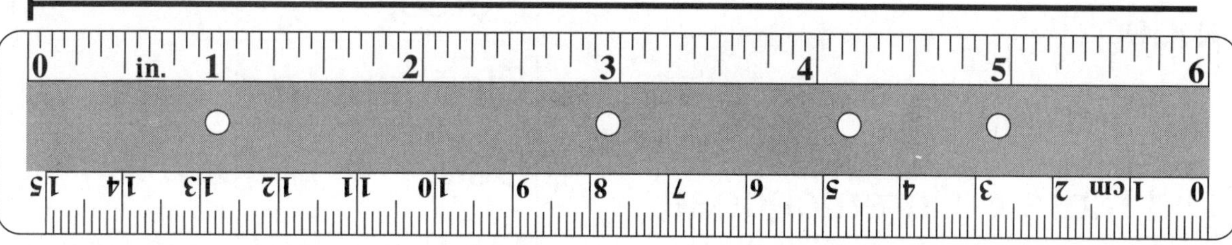

8. 2 inches

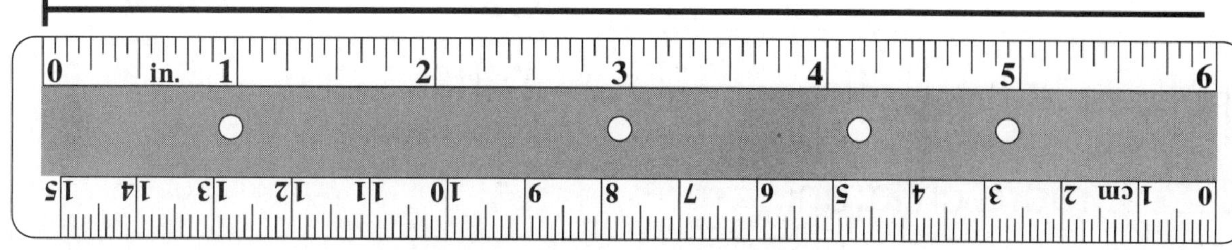

Name Date

Practice Set 36

How many units?

1. 

_____ units

2. 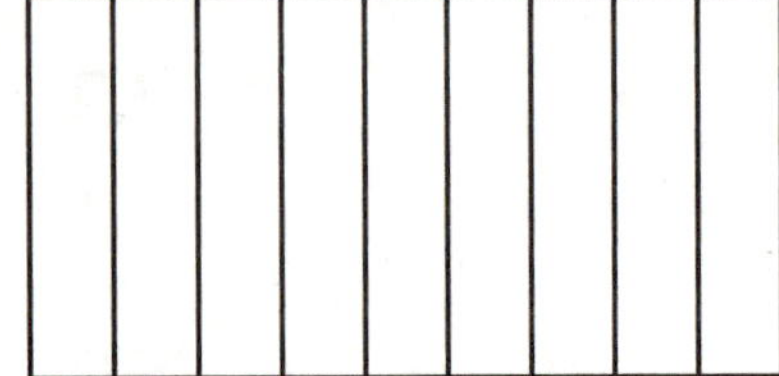

_____ units

3. 

_____ units

4. 

_____ units

Answer each question.

5. How many children chose a dog?

_____ children

6. Did more children choose a horse or a monkey?

____

How many more?

_____ more children

Favorite Animal	
Horse	///
Elephant	~~////~~
Dog	~~////~~ ~~////~~ ~~////~~ /
Monkey	~~////~~ ~~////~~ //
Cat	~~////~~ ~~////~~ //
Turtle	//

Use with or after Lesson 5.4.

Name Date

Practice Set 37

Write the total weight.

1.

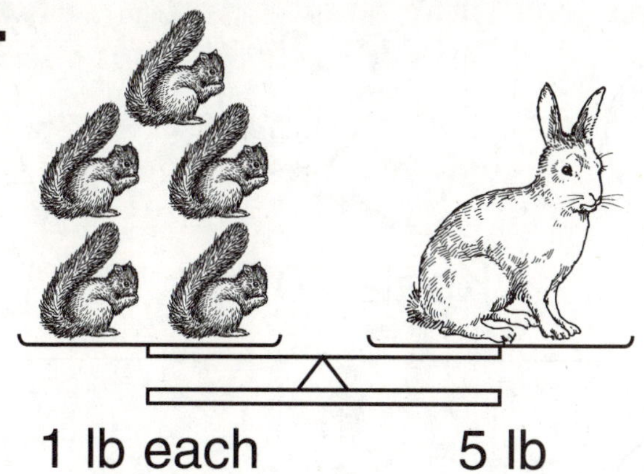

1 lb each 5 lb

_____ **pounds**

2.

300 lb 50 lb

_____ **pounds**

Count by 10s.

Unit
spiders

3. 70, ___, ___, 100, ___, ___, ___, ___, ___

4. 160, ___, 180, ___, ___, ___, ___, ___, ___

5. 36, 46, ___, ___, ___, ___, ___, 106, ___

6. 92, 102, ___, ___, ___, ___, ___, ___, ___

7. ___, 34, ___, ___, 64, ___, ___, ___, ___

8. ___, ___, 29, ___, ___, 59, ___, ___, ___

Name Date

Practice Set 38

Use < for *less than,* > for *more than,* or = for *equal to.*

1.

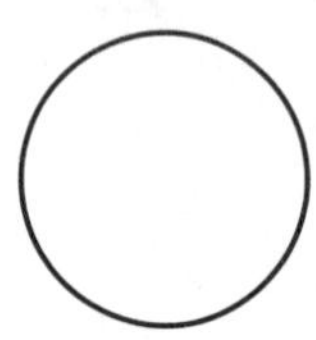

Raccoon 15 lb

Koala 20 lb

2.

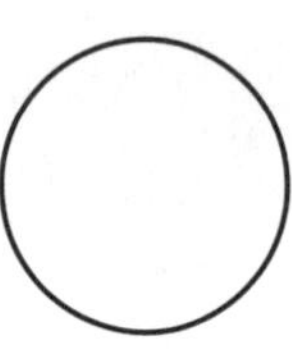

Beaver 56 lb

Girl 50 lb

3.

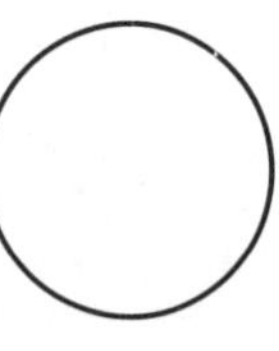

Five Squirrels 1 lb each

Rabbit 5 lb

4.

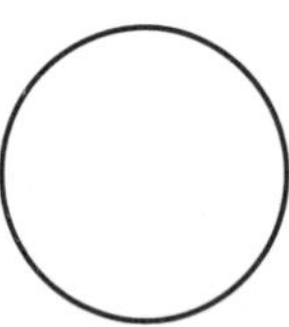

Raccoon 15 lb

Fox 14 lb

5.

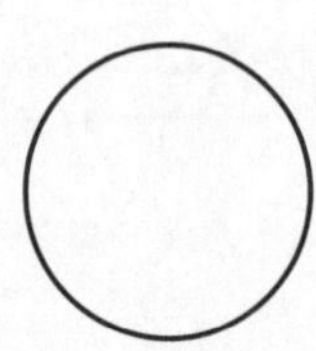

Black Bear 300 lb

Two Children
50 lb each

Use with or after Lesson 5.6.

Name Date

Practice Set 39

How many more?

Example

3 more pennies

1.

_____ more pennies

2.

_____ more pennies

Write >, <, or =.

3. 10 ☐ 20

4. 17 ☐ 17

5. 59 ☐ 69

6. 56 ☐ 57

< means *is less than*

> means *is greater than*

= means *is equal to*

Make these true.

Example 14 < 20

7. 18 > ☐

8. 30 > ☐

9. ☐ < 14

10. 103 > ☐

11. 9 = ☐ + ☐

Name Date

Practice Set 40

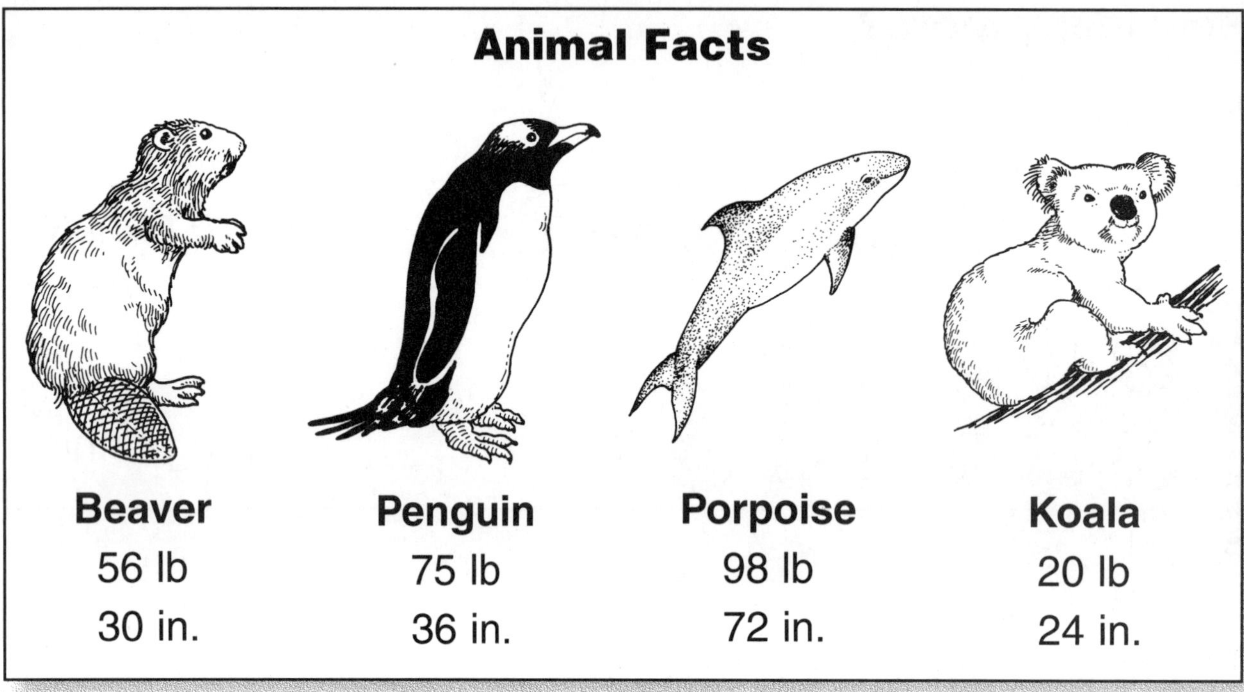

Solve each problem.

1. Which is longer, the beaver or the penguin?

   ____

   How much longer? ______________________ inches longer

2. Which weighs more, a beaver and a koala or a penguin?

   ____

3. Which weighs more, 2 beavers or a porpoise?

   ____

4. How much do a beaver and a koala weigh together?

   ______________________ pounds

 Use with or after Lesson 5.8.

Name Date

Practice Set 41

1. Match the turn-around facts.

4 + 3 = 7	5 + 4 = 9
6 + 4 = 10	3 + 4 = 7
4 + 5 = 9	4 + 6 = 10

Write the turn-around fact.

2. 8 + 1 = 9

____ + ____ = ____

3. 3 + 5 = 8

____ + ____ = ____

4. 2 + 9 = 11

____ + ____ = ____

5. 6 + 1 = 7

____ + ____ = ____

6. How many pennies make 1 dime? Circle (penny)s.

Write the number that is 10 more.

Example 15, 25 **7.** 26, ____ **8.** 51, ____

9. 69, ____ **10.** 82, ____ **11.** 9, ____

Name Date

Practice Set 42

Add.

Unit
snakes

1. 3 + 0 = ____

2. 4 + 0 = ____

3. 5 + 0 = ____

4. 6 + 0 = ____

5. 7 + 0 = ____

6. 8 + 0 = ____

7. 4 + 1 = ____

8. 5 + 1 = ____

9. 6 + 1 = ____

10. 7 + 1 = ____

11. 8 + 1 = ____

12. 9 + 1 = ____

Answer each question.

13. How many children are 44 inches tall? ____ children

14. How many children are 46 inches tall? ____ children

15. How many more children are 44 inches tall than 46 inches tall?

____ more children

First Grade Heights (inches)	
42	~~////~~
43	~~////~~ ~~////~~ ~~////~~ /
44	~~////~~ ~~////~~ /
45	~~////~~ //
46	////
47	//

Use with or after Lesson 5.11.

Name Date

Practice Set 43

"What's My Rule?"

1.

in

Rule

1 more

out

in	out
2	3
3	4
4	
5	
6	

2.

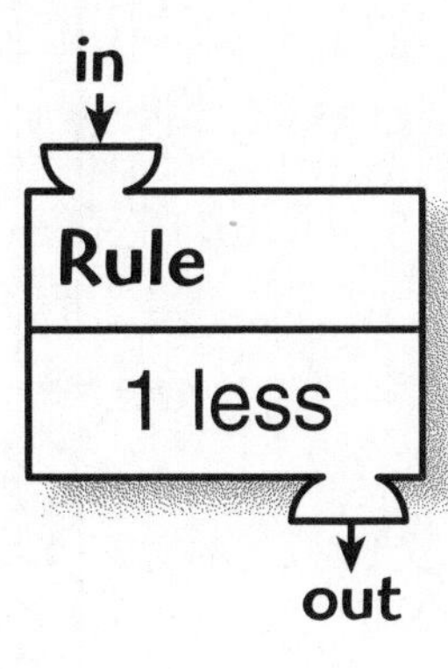

in	out
7	6
8	
9	
10	
11	

Circle *odd* or *even.*

3. 

odd **even**

4. 

odd **even**

5. 

odd **even**

6. 

odd **even**

Fill in the missing numbers. Count down.

7. 29, ____, ____, 26, ____, ____, ____, ____, ____, ____

Name Date

Practice Set 44

Circle the names that DO belong.

1. **12**

6 + 6   7 + 3

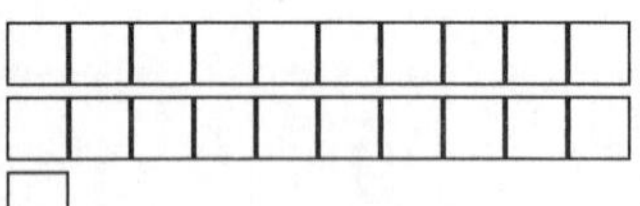

15 − 4   20 − 8

2. **9**

/ + / + / + / + / + / + / + / + /

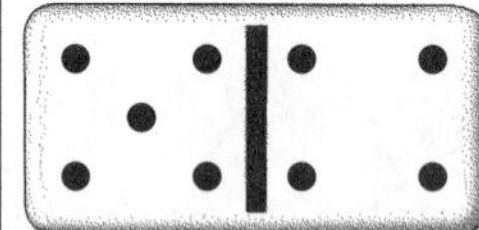

9 + 0   8 + 2

Add.

3. 1 + 1 = ______ **4.** 2 + 2 = ______ **5.** 3 + 3 = ______

6. 4 + 4 = ______ **7.** 5 + 5 = ______ **8.** 6 + 6 = ______

9. 7 + 7 = ______ **10.** 8 + 8 = ______ **11.** 9 + 9 = ______

"What's My Rule?"

12.

in	out
3	4
6	
9	
1	
7	

13.

in	out
4	6
5	
6	
7	
8	

Use with or after Lesson 6.2.

Name Date

Practice Set 45

Write 3 numbers for each domino.

1. 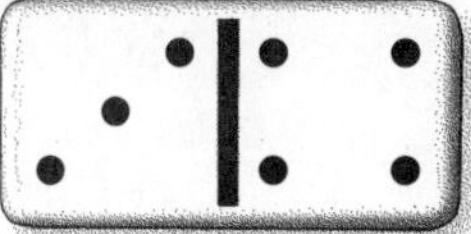

___, ___, ___

2. 

___, ___, ___

3. 

___, ___, ___

4. 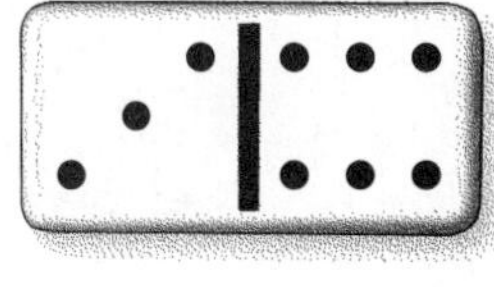

___, ___, ___

5. 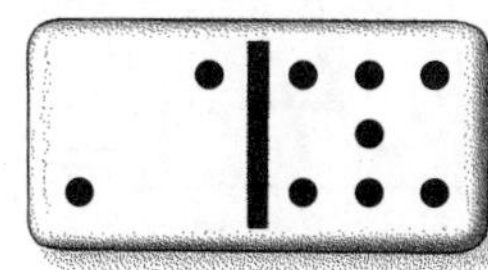

___, ___, ___

6. 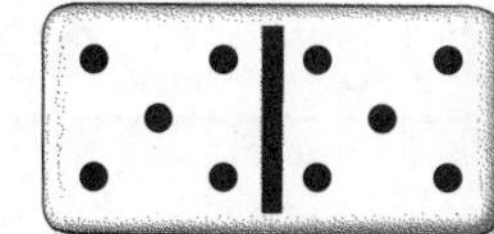

___, ___, ___

Fill in the frames.

7. Rule: Count by 10s

13, 23, ☐, ☐, ☐

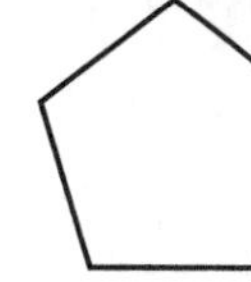
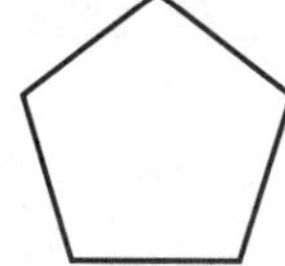
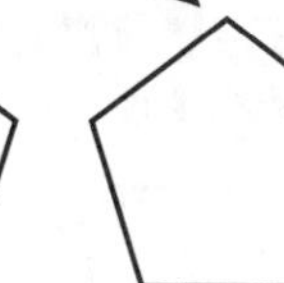

8. Rule: Add 5

8, 13, ⬠, ⬠, ⬠

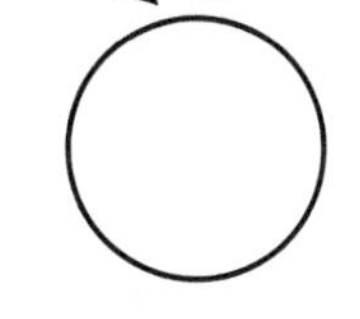
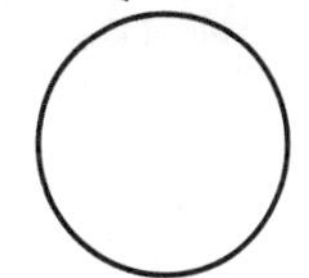
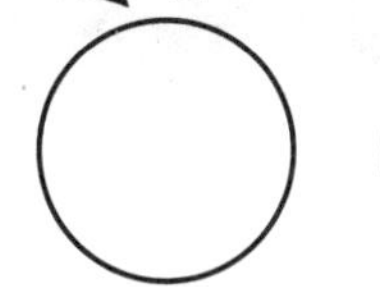

9. Rule: Subtract 2

40, ○, ○, ○, ○

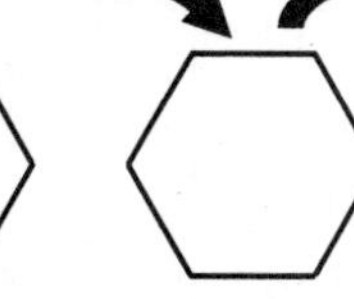
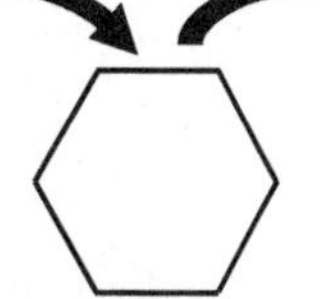
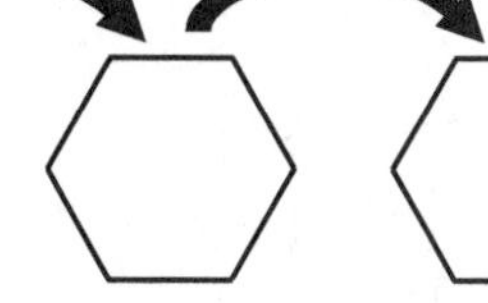

10. Rule: Subtract 3

18, ⬡, ⬡, ⬡, ⬡

Name Date

Practice Set 46

Write the fact family for the Fact Triangle.

Example

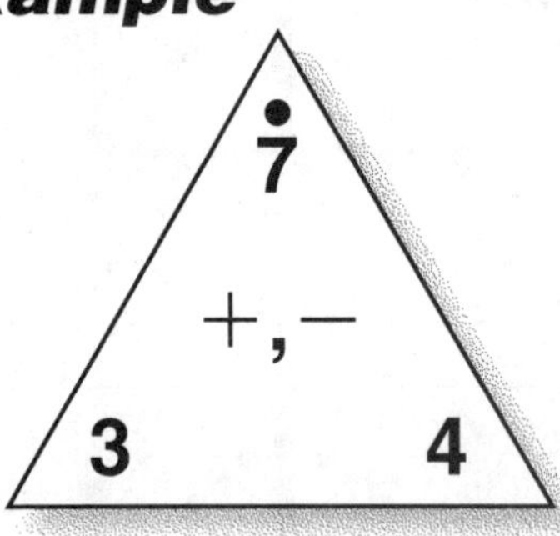

7 = 3 + 4

7 = 4 + 3

7 − 3 = 4

7 − 4 = 3

1.

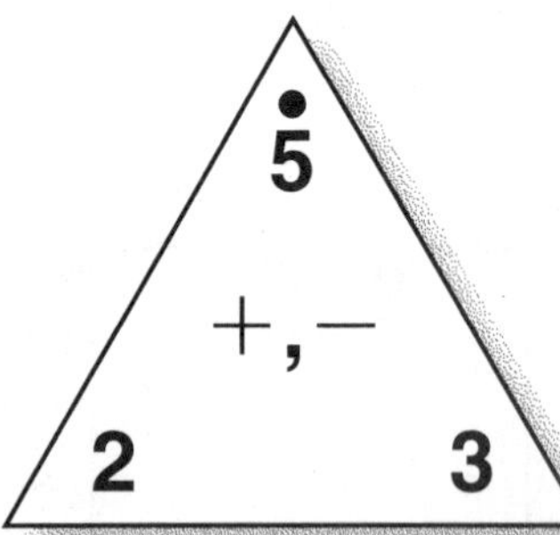

5 = ______ + ______

5 = ______ + ______

5 − ______ = ______

5 − ______ = ______

How much money?

2.

\$0.______ or ______¢

3.

\$0.______ or ______¢

Use with or after Lesson 6.4.

Name Date

Practice Set 47

Measure each line segment. Use centimeters.

1.

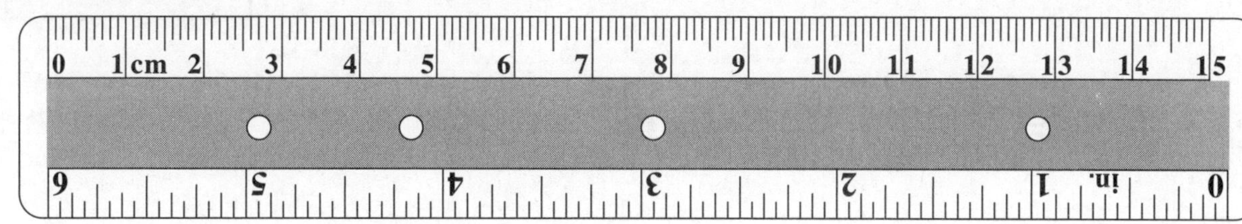

= about ________ centimeters

2.

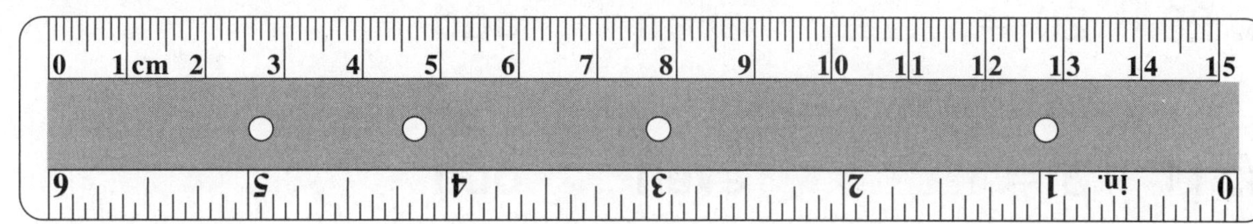

= about ________ centimeters

3.

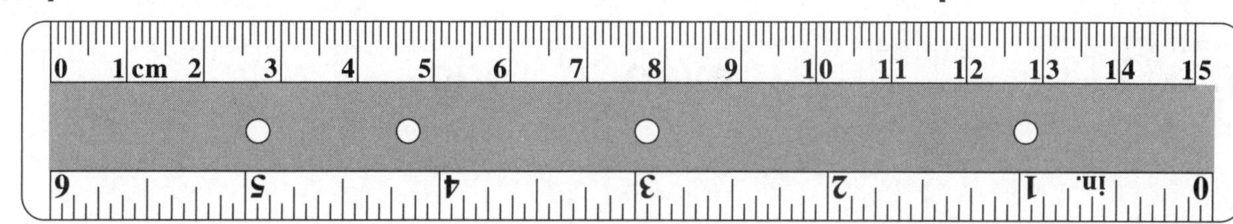

= about ________ centimeters

Write the missing numbers.

	Before	Number	After
Example	49	50	51
4.		32	
5.	21		23

	Before	Number	After
6.		14	15
7.		60	
8.	39	40	

Name Date

Practice Set 48

Find the sum. Then circle *even* or *odd*.

Unit
books

1. 2 + 3 = ______ **even** **odd**

2. 4 + 5 = ______ **even** **odd**

3. 10 + 10 = ______ **even** **odd**

4. 20 + 20 = ______ **even** **odd**

5. 11 + 3 = ______ **even** **odd**

6. 100 + 1 = ______ **even** **odd**

7. $\begin{array}{r} 7 \\ +\ 3 \\ \hline \end{array}$ **even** **odd**

8. $\begin{array}{r} 4 \\ +\ 2 \\ \hline \end{array}$ **even** **odd**

9. $\begin{array}{r} 7 \\ +\ 4 \\ \hline \end{array}$ **even** **odd**

10. $\begin{array}{r} 9 \\ +\ 2 \\ \hline \end{array}$ **even** **odd**

Use with or after Lesson 6.7.

Name Date

Practice Set 49

"What's My Rule?" Fill in the blanks.

1.

in

Rule

Add 5

out

in	out
5	
10	
25	
15	
30	

2.

in

Rule

Add 2

out

in	out
	7
	25
	16
	73
	39

What time is it?

3.

quarter-to ______

4.

half-past ______

Write another name for the number.

5. 15 ______________

6. 27 ______________

Name Date

Practice Set 50

How much money?

1.  

$0.______

2.  

______¢

3.  

______¢

4.  

$0.______

Use your calculator. Count by 5s.

Press (ON/C) (5) (+) (5) (=) (=) (=) (=)

5. 5, 10, 15, 20, ___, ___, ___, ___, ___,

___, ___, ___, ___, ___, ___, ___, ___, ___,

___, ___, ___, ___, ___, ___, ___, ___, ___

 Use with or after Lesson 6.9.

Name Date

Practice Set 51

Match the clocks.

Example

1.

2.

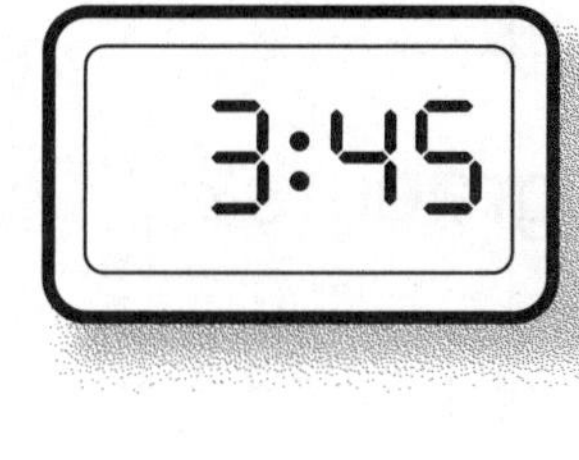

3.

Write 3 numbers for each domino.

4. 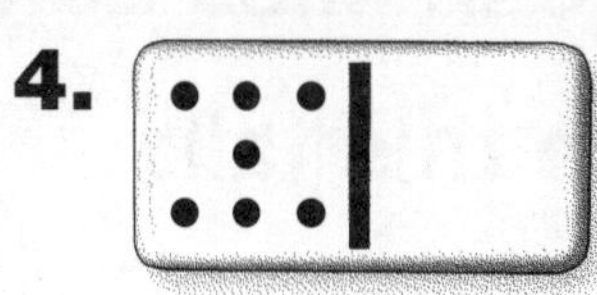

_____, _____, _____

5.

_____, _____, _____

6. 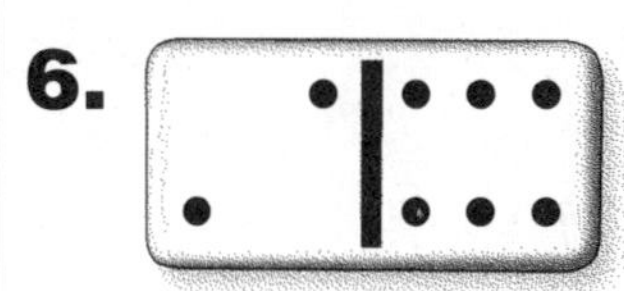

_____, _____, _____

7.

_____, _____, _____

8.

_____, _____, _____

Name Date

Practice Set 52

The children are in first grade.

They are in Miss Lund's reading group.

They are this tall:

Sally	Kendra	Drew	Ken	Lorna
41 in.	46 in.	46 in.	46 in.	49 in.

1. What is the **difference** between the largest number and the smallest number?

$$\begin{array}{r} 49 \\ -\ 41 \\ \hline \end{array}$$

2. What is the **range**? ______

3. About how tall are first graders?

   They are about ______ inches tall.

Fill in the five-minute marks.

4.

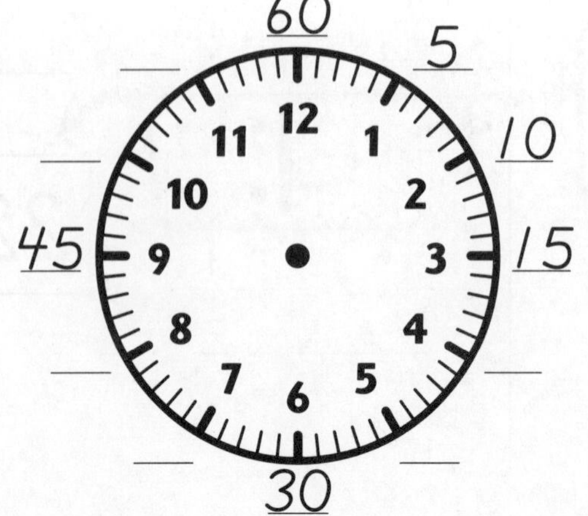

5.

Use with or after Lesson 6.12.

Name Date

Practice Set 53

1. Circle the triangles.

 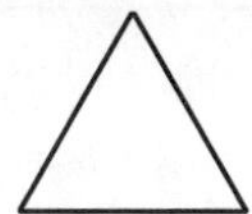 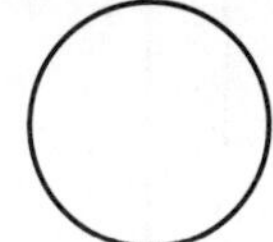 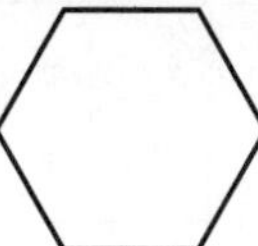 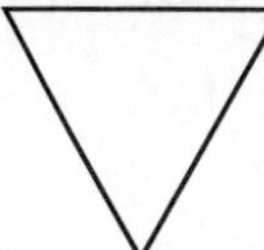 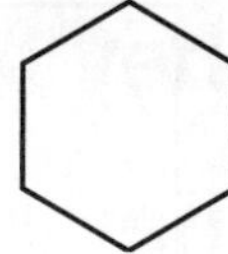

2. Circle the squares.

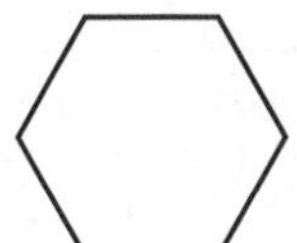 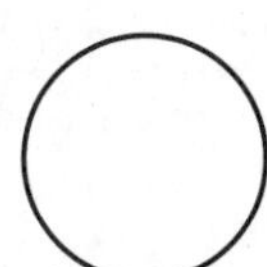 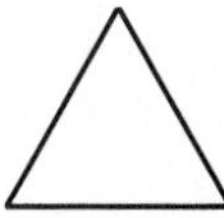 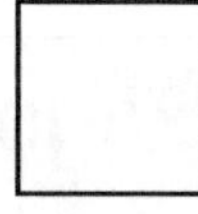 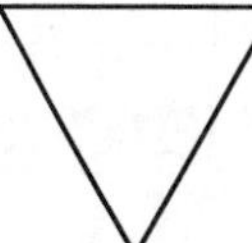 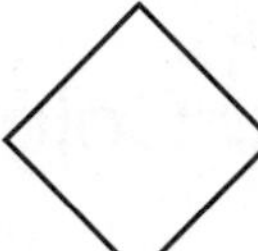

Fill in the rule box.

Example

Rule
Count down by 1s

17 16 15 14 13

3.

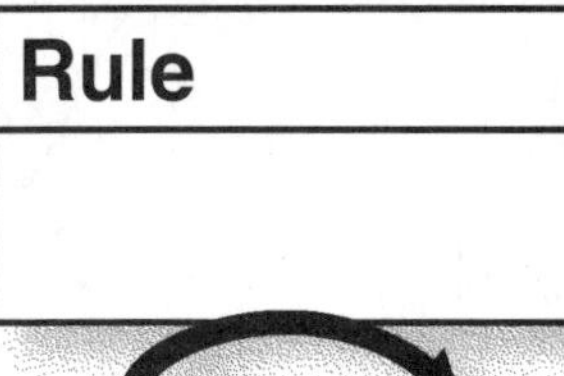

Rule

25 27 29 31 33

4.

Rule

10 13 16 19 22

Name Date

Practice Set 54

1. Color the smallest rectangle.

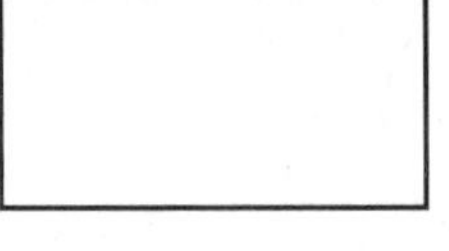

2. Color the largest hexagon.

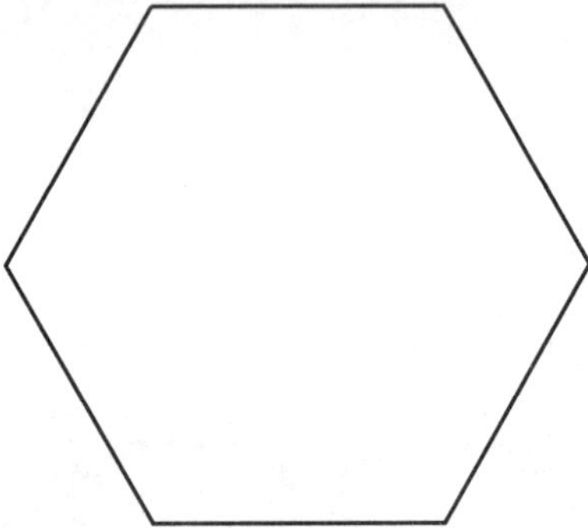
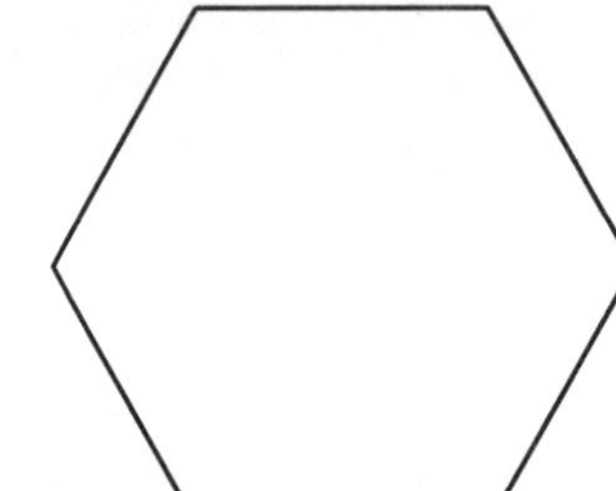
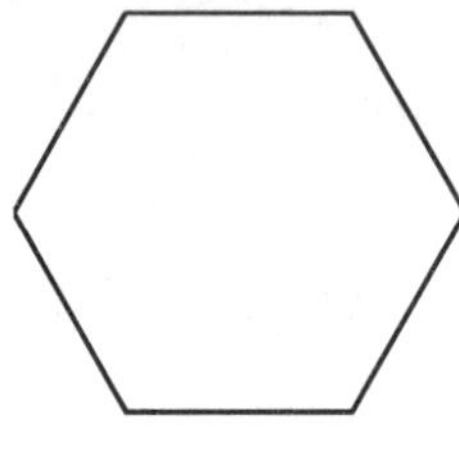

List the fact family for the Fact Triangle.

Example

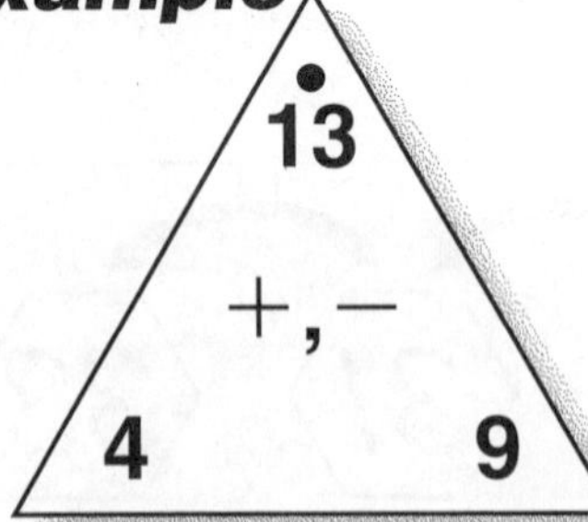

4 + 9 = 13
9 + 4 = 13
13 − 4 = 9
13 − 9 = 4

3.

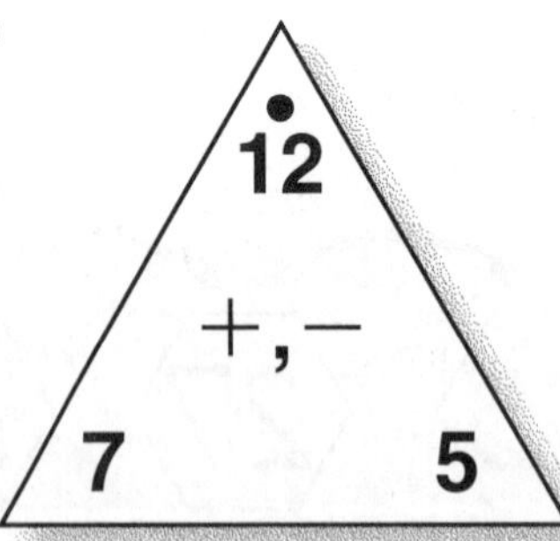

______
______
______
______

4.

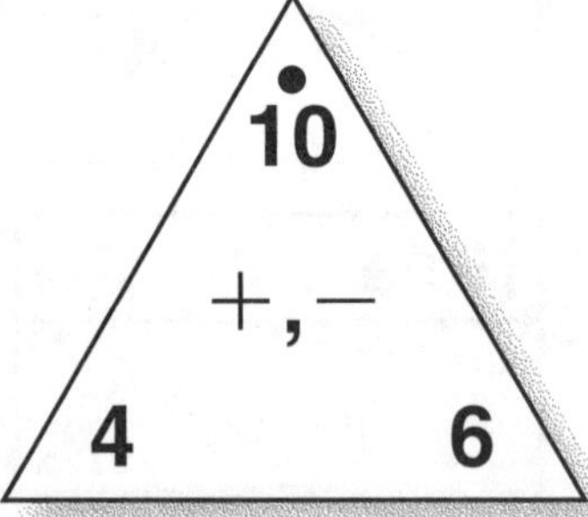

______
______
______
______

Name Date

Practice Set 55

Color the one that is the same size and shape.

1.

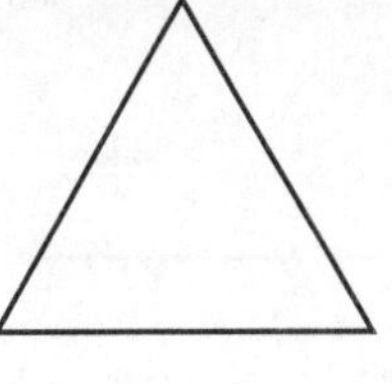

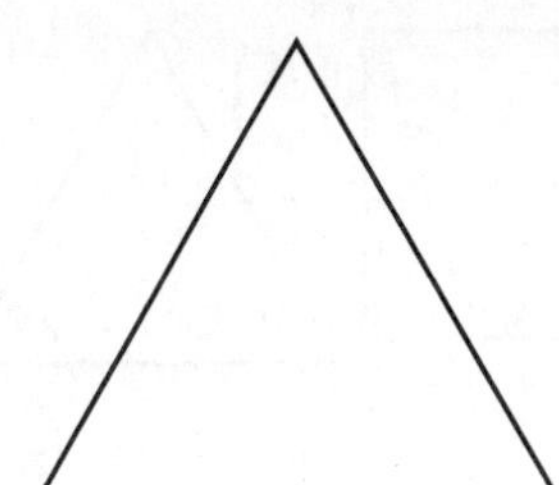

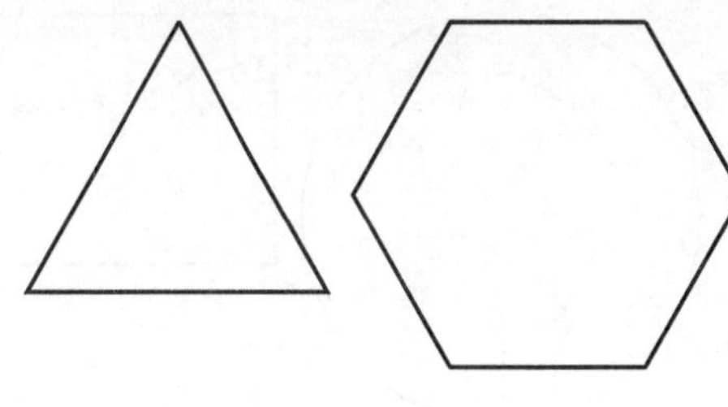

2.

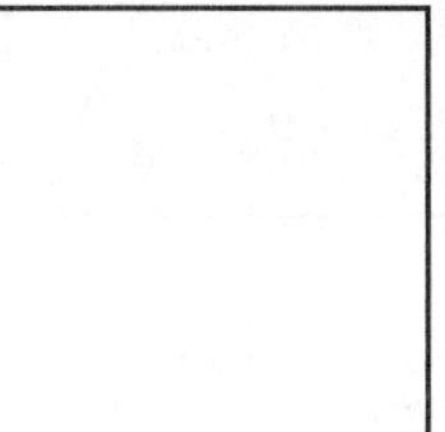

What time is it? Circle the correct time.

3.

5:40

6:40

6:20

4.

3:15

2:15

2:45

5.

12:05

12:10

12:15

6.

7:25

7:35

7:45

Name Date

Practice Set 56

1. Color all of the 4-sided polygons.

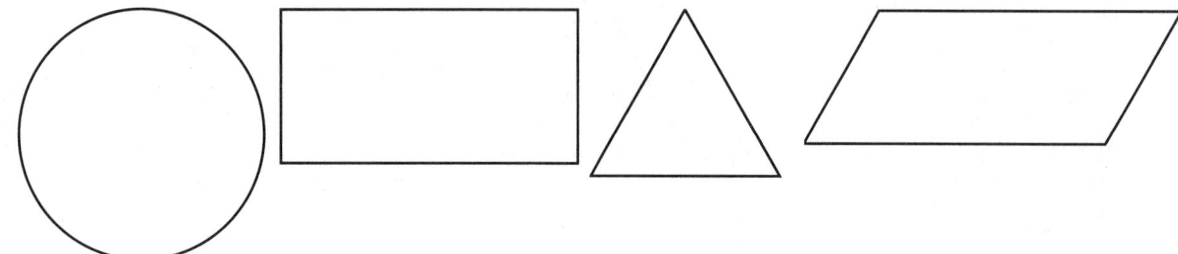

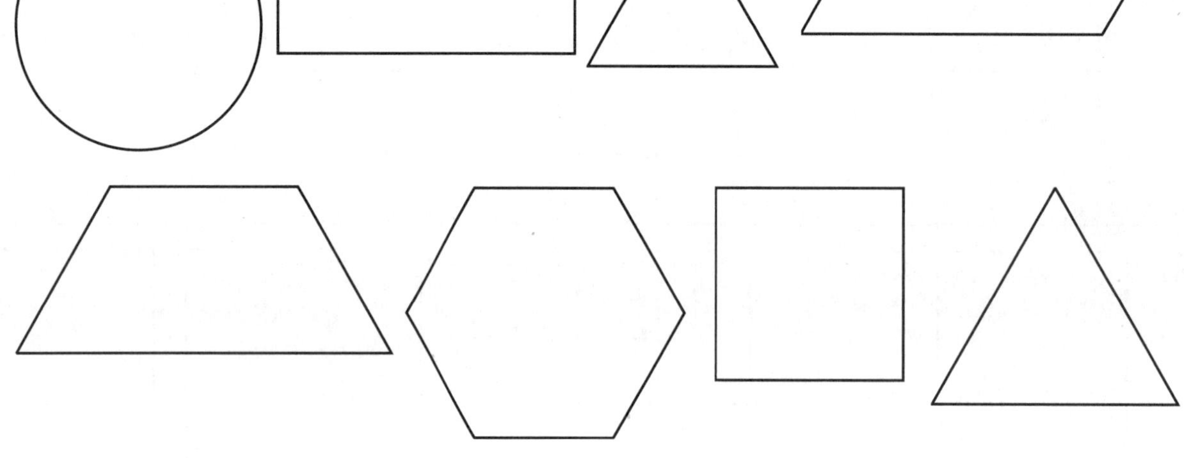

Complete the number family.

2.

3 Family	
0	3

3.

5 Family	
2	3

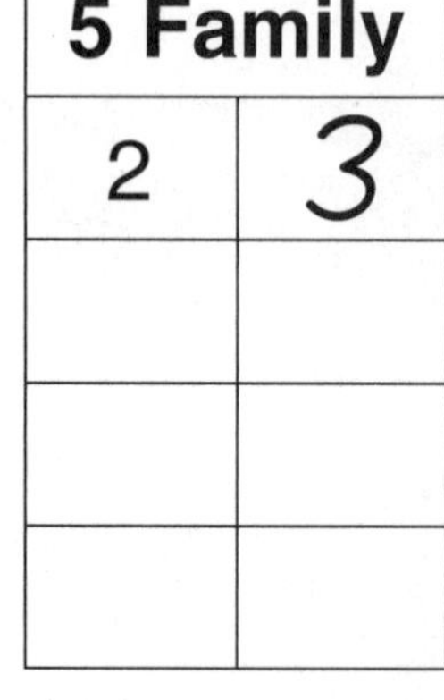

Write the number that is 10 more.

4. 64, ____ **5.** 39, ____ **6.** 41, ____

Write the number that is 10 less.

7. ____, 99 **8.** ____, 27 **9.** ____, 53

Name Date

Practice Set 57

1. Circle the one that will roll.

How many flat faces? How many corners?

2.

____ flat faces

____ corners

3.

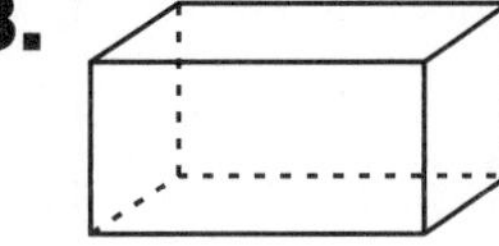

____ flat faces

____ corners

4. Circle those that are true.

$3 + 7 = 7 + 3$ $6 - 5 = 5 - 6$

$4 = 2 + 3$ $3 + 1 = 4$

Write 3 numbers for each domino.

5.

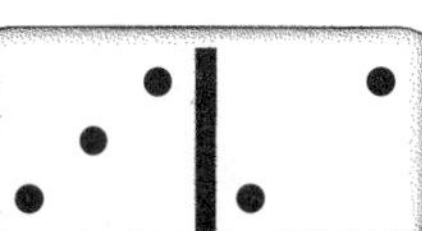

____, ____, ____

6.

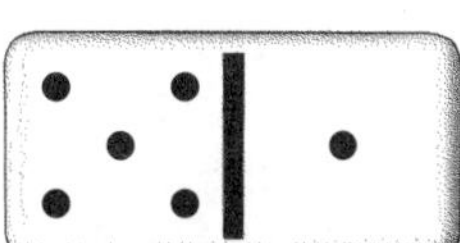

____, ____, ____

7.

____, ____, ____

8.

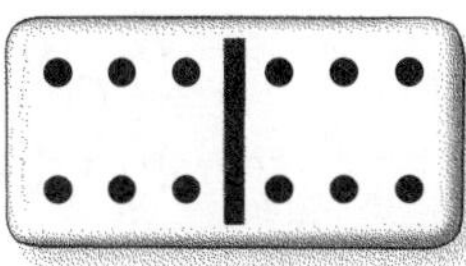
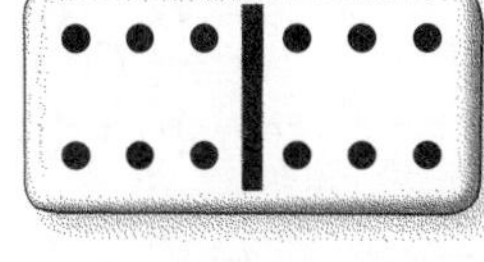

____, ____, ____

9.

____, ____, ____

10.

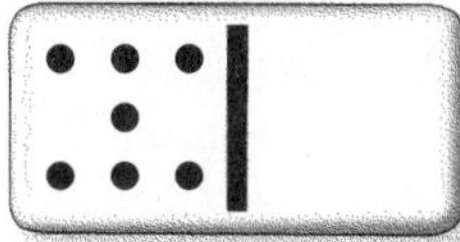
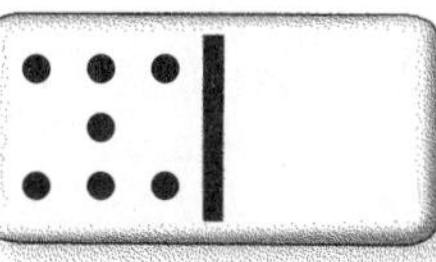

____, ____, ____

Name Date

Practice Set 58

What shape can you make using the ink pad?

Example

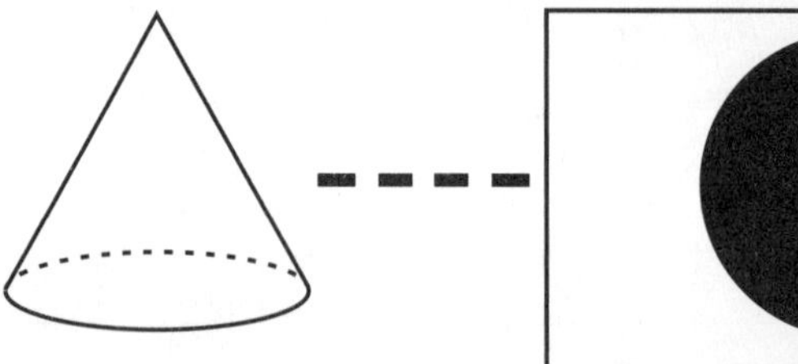

1.

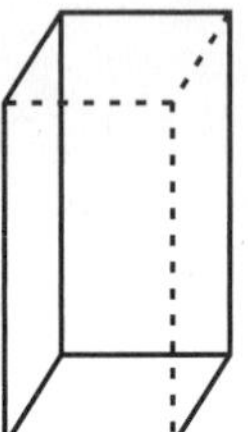

2.

Fill in the rule box and the blanks.

3.

in	out
10	8
6	4
	10
14	
	7

4.

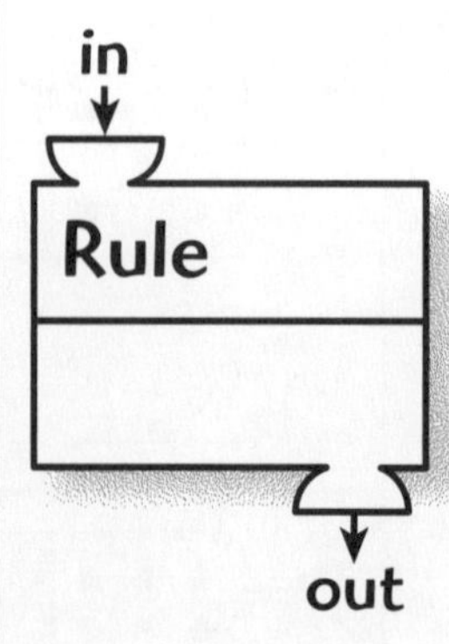

in	out
3	7
7	11
5	
	10
	12

Name Date

Practice Set 59

What will the shape look like after you cut it out and open it up? Draw a line to match.

1.

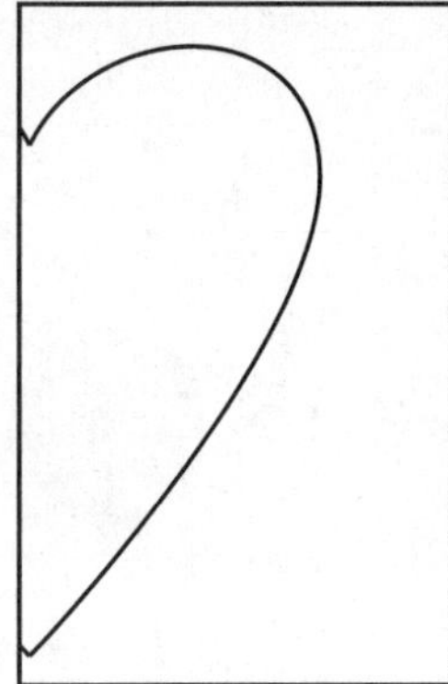

2.

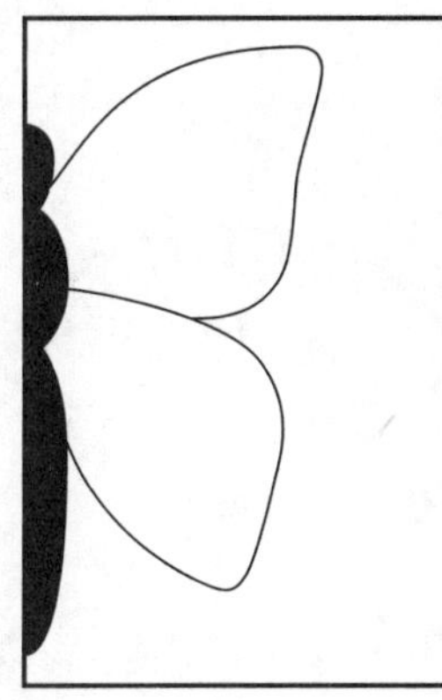

---

3. Show 35 cents two different ways.

Name Date

Practice Set 60

How many?

1. 25  = ____ 

2. 2  = ____ 

3. ____  = 1 

4. ____  = 15 

Draw hands to show the time.

5. 

8:25

6. 

5:45

7. 

12:10

Fill in the unit box.
Then write the missing numbers.

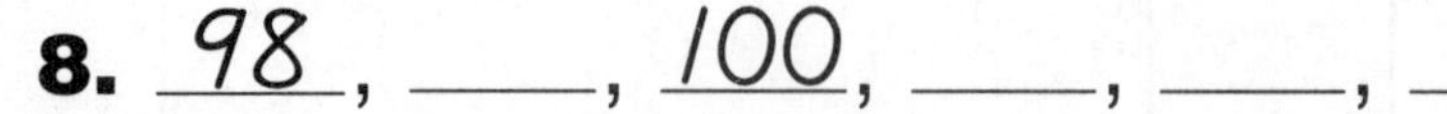

8. 98, ____, 100, ____, ____, ____, ____, ____

9. 112, ____, ____, 115, ____, ____, ____, ____

Use with or after Lesson 8.1.

Name Date

Practice Set 61

Write the amount.

Example one dollar and sixty-two cents $1.62

1. three dollars and fourteen cents ______

2. two dollars and seven cents ______

3. one dollar and ninety-one cents ______

4. eighty-nine cents ______

Write the missing number.

5. ____ pennies = 1 dollar

6. 1 dollar = ____ dimes

7. 1 dollar = ____ quarters

8. 20 nickels = ____ dollar

9. 1 dollar = ____ quarters and ____ dimes

Complete the number family.

10.

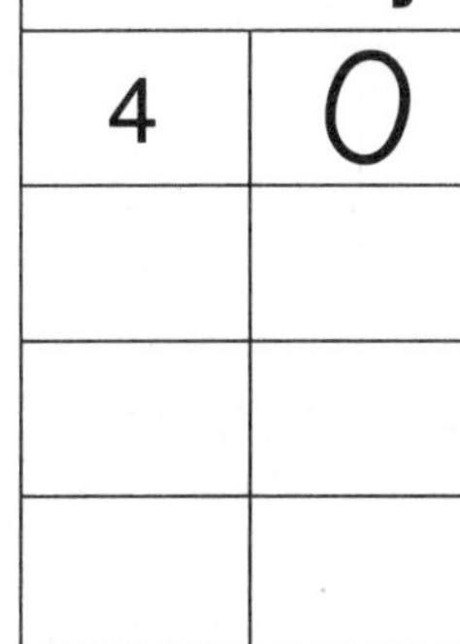

4 Family	
4	0

11.

5 Family	
2	3

Name Date

Practice Set 62

What number do the blocks show?

1.

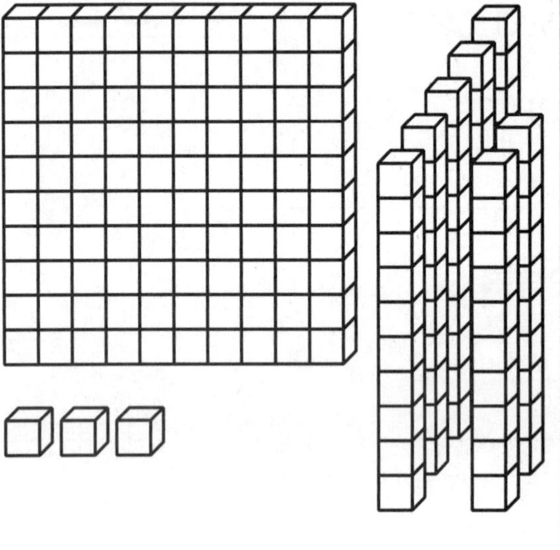

____

2.

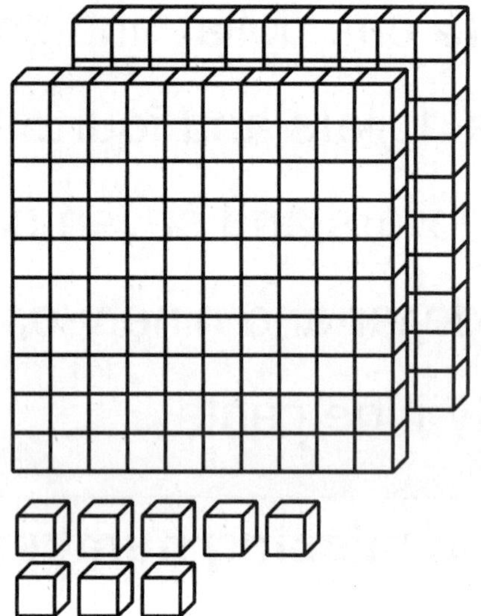

____

Fill in the missing numbers.

3.

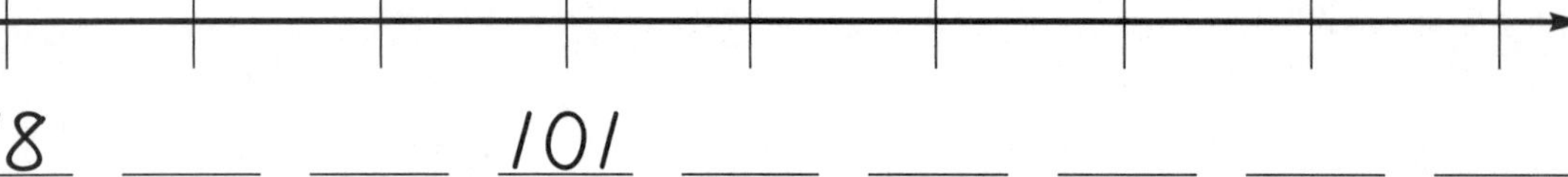

98 ____ ____ 101 ____ ____ ____ ____ ____

4.

131 ____ ____ ____ 135 ____ ____ ____ ____

5.

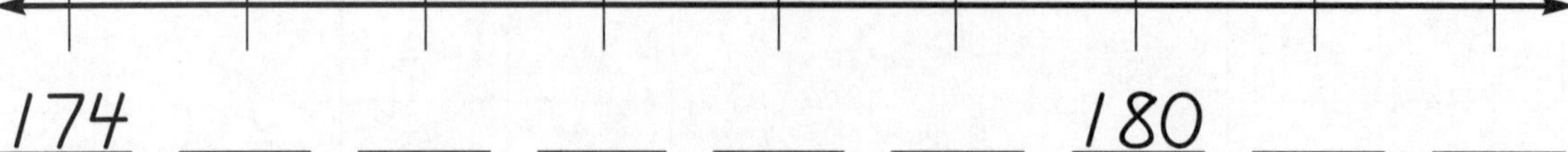

174 ____ ____ ____ ____ ____ 180 ____ ____

6.

198 ____ ____ ____ ____ 203 ____ ____ ____

 Use with or after Lesson 8.3.

Name Date

Practice Set 63

Toy Store

ball	ring	crayons	bear
$0.20	12¢	$0.25	16¢

Solve each number story.

1. How much do 2 rings cost? $0._____ or _____ ¢

2. How much do a bear and a ball cost? $0._____ or _____ ¢

3. Which costs more, crayons or a ball?

____

How much more? $0._____ or _____ ¢ more

4. How much do crayons and a bear cost?

$0._____ or _____ ¢

5. Write a number story about the Toy Store.

____

____

____

____

Name Date

Practice Set 64

How much change?

1.

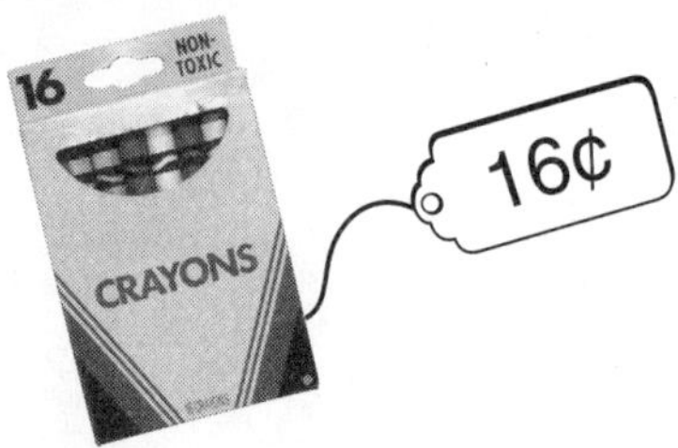

____

2.

____

Write the addition turn-around facts.

Example

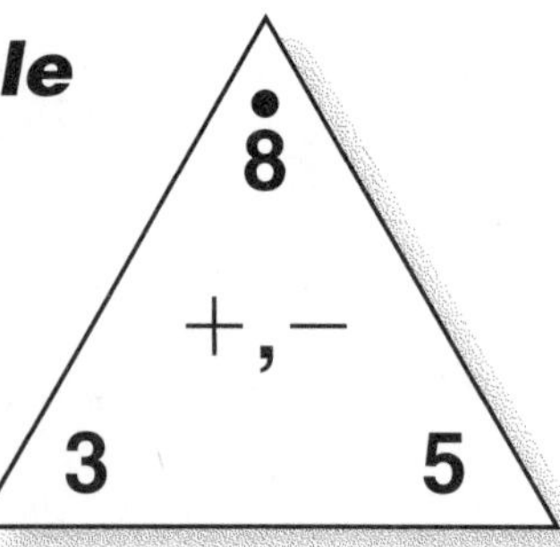

3 + 5 = 8

5 + 3 = 8

3.

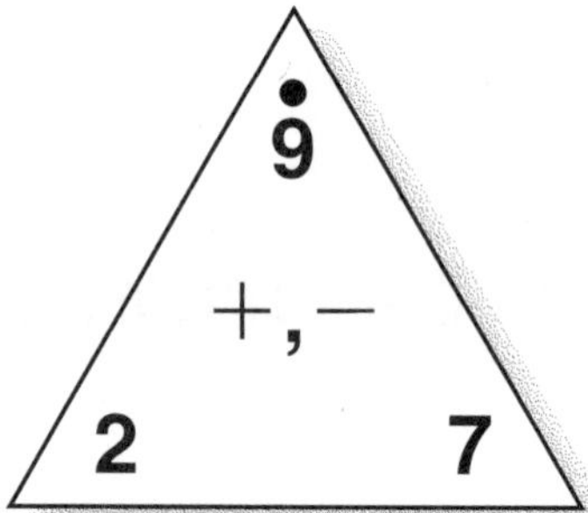

____

____

4.

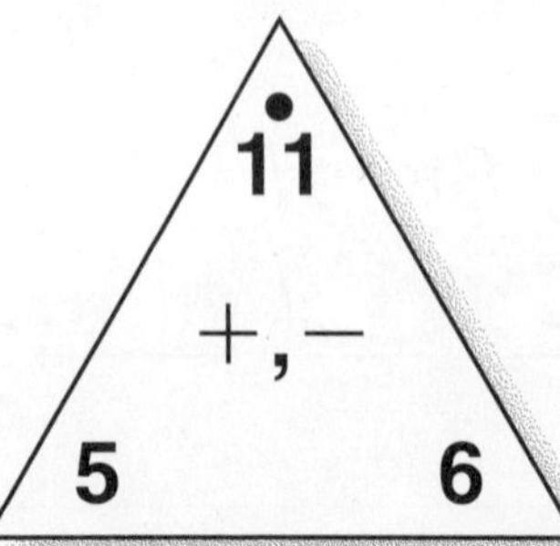

____

____

5.

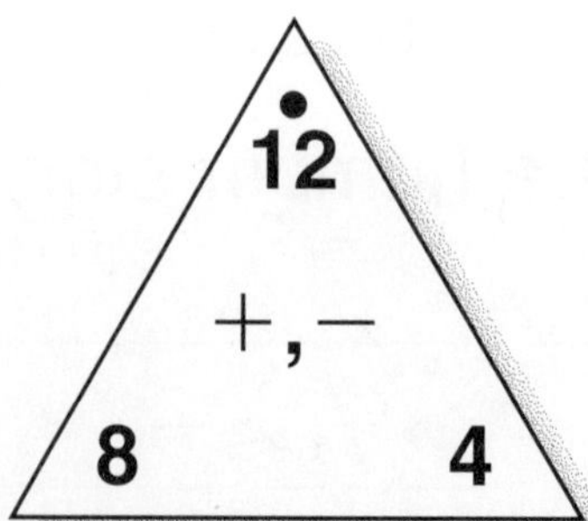

____

____

Name Date

Practice Set 65

Write the fraction for the shaded part.

Example

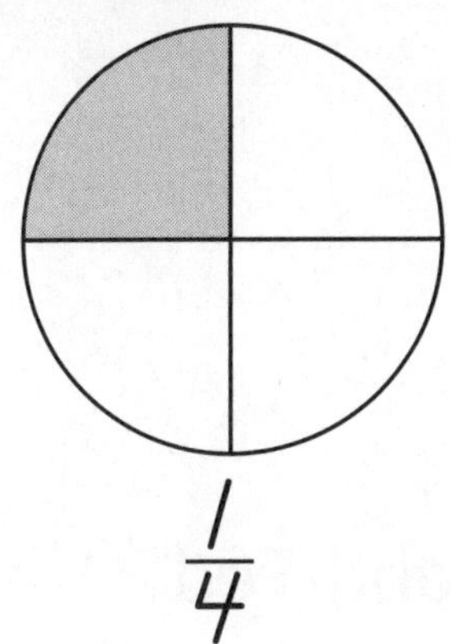

1/4

1.

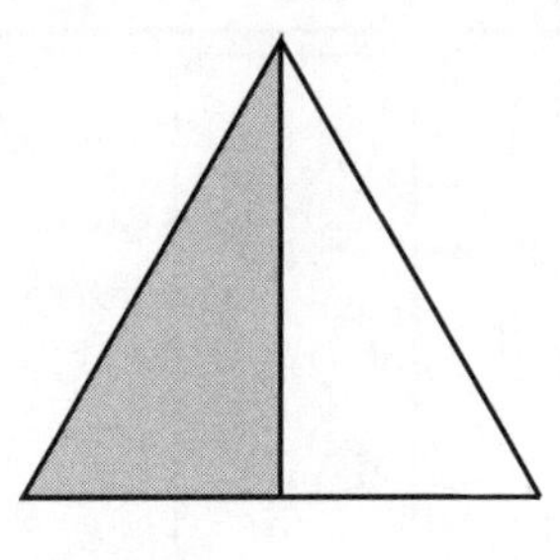

2.

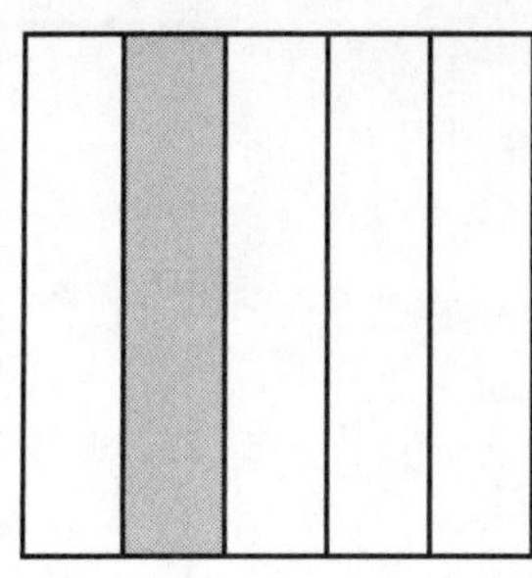

3.

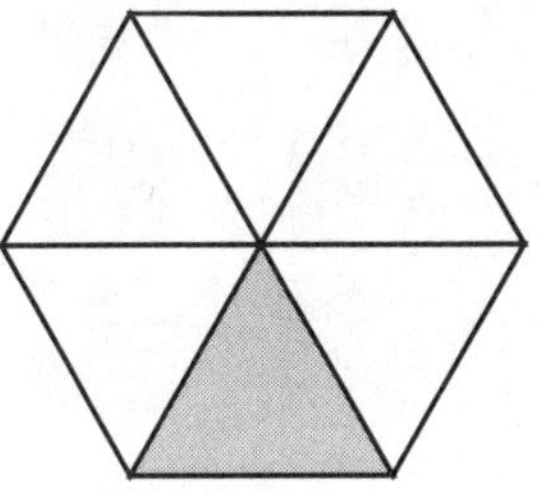

4.

5.

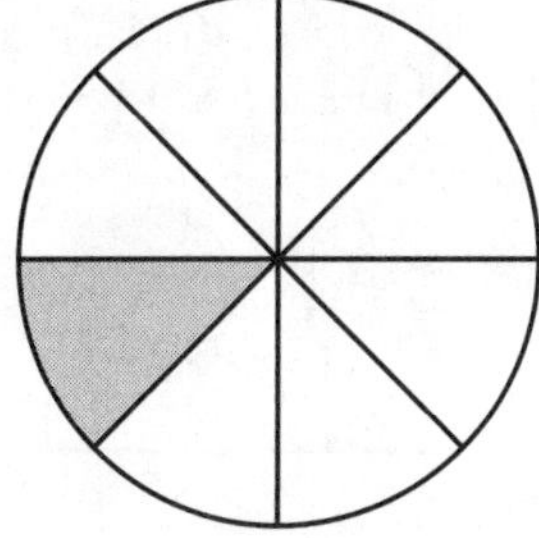

Fill in the unit box. Then find each sum.

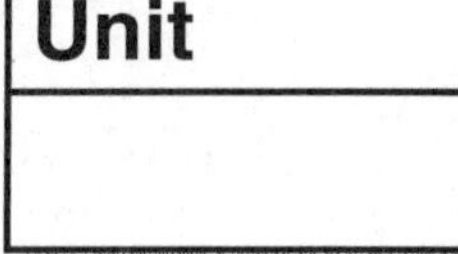

6. ____ = 5 + 6 **7.** 7 + 3 = ____

8. 9 + 9 = ____ **9.** ____ = 6 + 9 **10.** ____ = 4 + 5

11. 7 + 7 **12.** 8 + 4 **13.** 9 + 3 **14.** 2 + 8 **15.** 4 + 9

Name Date

Practice Set 66

How many pennies will each person get?

Example Marcus and Albert

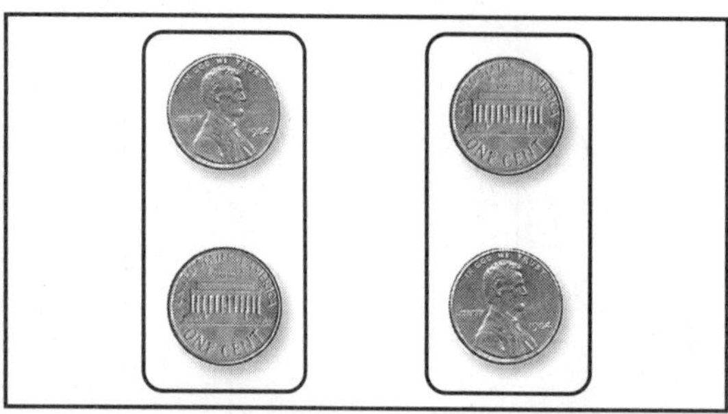

1. Sandy and Brenda

2. Tim, Tom, and Ted

Write a 3-digit number.

Example

4 in the hundreds place
7 in the tens place
2 in the ones place
472

3. 9 in the hundreds place
1 in the tens place
6 in the ones place
______

4. 3 in the hundreds place
8 in the tens place
5 in the ones place
______

5. 2 in the hundreds place
0 in the tens place
4 in the ones place
______

Use with or after Lesson 8.8.

Name Date

Practice Set 67

1. Count by 10s. Start at 6.
Write an **X** over each number you count.

									0
1	2	3	4	5	6 (X)	7	8	9	10
11	12	13	14	15	16 (X)	17	18	19	20
21	22	23	24	25	26	27	28	29	30
31	32	33	34	35	36	37	38	39	40
41	42	43	44	45	46	47	48	49	50
51	52	53	54	55	56	57	58	59	60
61	62	63	64	65	66	67	68	69	70
71	72	73	74	75	76	77	78	79	80
81	82	83	84	85	86	87	88	89	90
91	92	93	94	95	96	97	98	99	100
101	102	103	104	105	106	107	108	109	110
111	112	113	114	115	116	117	118	119	120

Fill in the unit box.
Then fill in the blanks.

Unit

Example 215 = 2 hundreds 1 ten 5 ones

2. 87 = ____tens ____ones

3. 394 = ____hundreds ____tens ____ones

4. 762 = ____hundreds ____tens ____ones

Name Date

Practice Set 68

"What's My Rule?" Fill in the blanks.
Use your number grid.

1.

Rule: Add 10

in	out
60	
83	
47	
162	
215	

2.

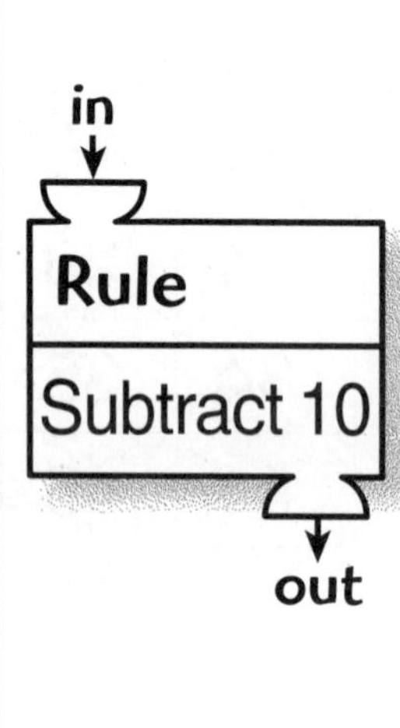

in	out
90	
76	
102	
210	
238	

Fill in the unit box. Then find each sum.

Unit

3. $5 + 3$

4. $6 + 4$

5. $3 + 2$

6. $5 + 0$

7. $8 + 5$

8. $9 + 1$

9. $3 + 6$

10. $4 + 7$

11. $4 + 2$

12. _____ $= 6 + 6$

13. $3 + 9 =$ _____

Use with or after Lesson 9.2.

Name Date

Practice Set 69

Fill in each number-grid piece below.

Example

14
24
34
44
54
64
74

−9	−8	−7	−6	−5	−4	−3	−2	−1	0
1	2	3	4	5	6	7	8	9	10
11	12	13	14	15	16	17	18	19	20
21	22	23	24	25	26	27	28	29	30
31	32	33	34	35	36	37	38	39	40
41	42	43	44	45	46	47	48	49	50
51	52	53	54	55	56	57	58	59	60
61	62	63	64	65	66	67	68	69	70
71	72	73	74	75	76	77	78	79	80
81	82	83	84	85	86	87	88	89	90
91	92	93	94	95	96	97	98	99	100
101	102	103	104	105	106	107	108	109	110

1.

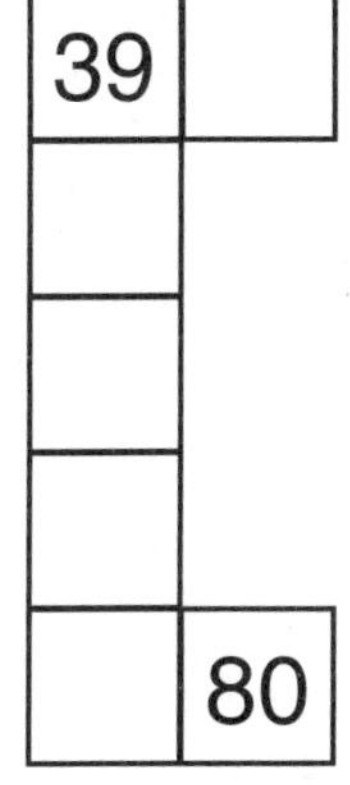

2.

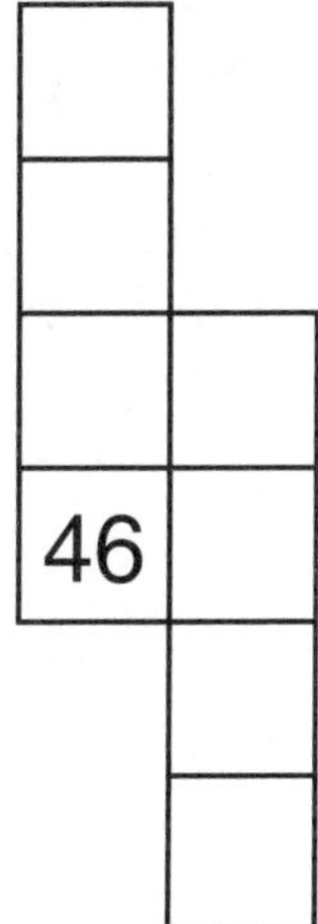

3.

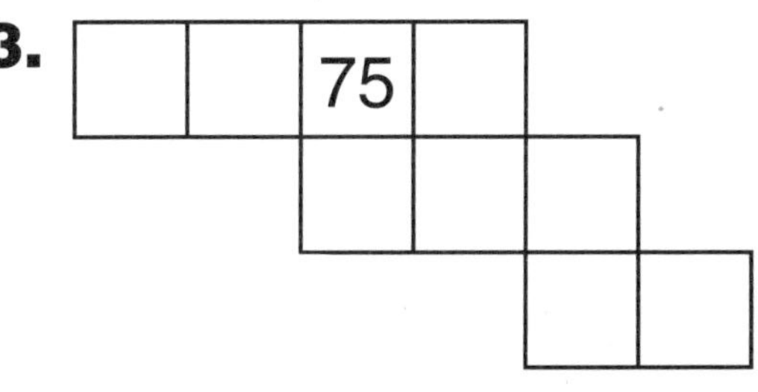

4.

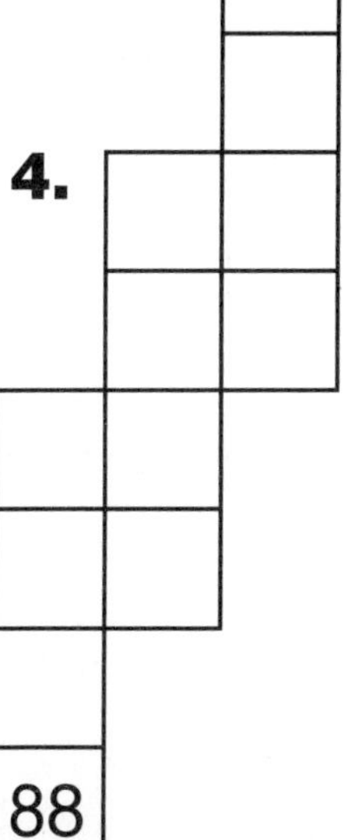

Name Date

Practice Set 70

Animal Facts

Fish	**Woodpecker**	**Black Bear**	**Fox**
15 oz	2 oz	300 lb	14 lb
12 in.	8 in.	60 in.	20 in.

Solve each problem.

1. Which is shorter, the fox or the fish?

____

How much shorter? ________ inches shorter

2. Which weighs less, the woodpecker or the fish?

____

How much less? ________ oz less

3. What is the total length of the fox and the black bear?

Their total length is __________ inches.

Name Date

Practice Set 71

1. Color one-half of the circle.

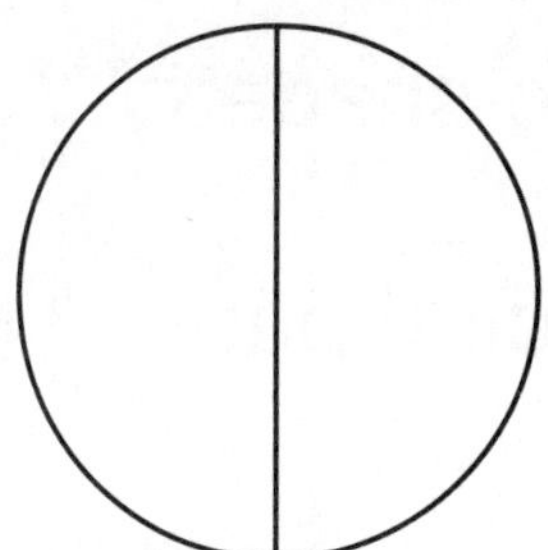

2. Color three-fourths of the square.

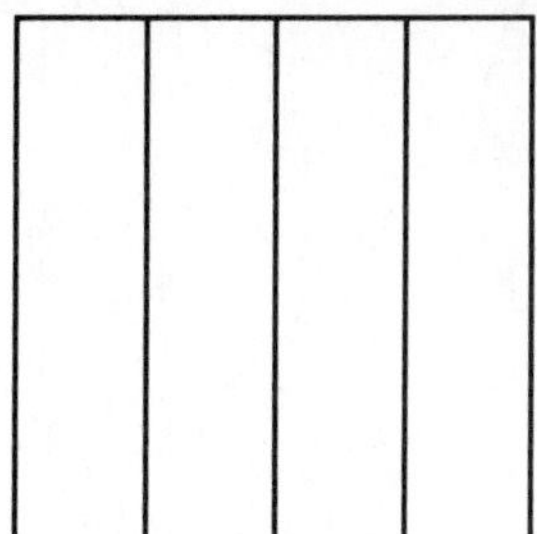

Fill in the rule box. Complete the frames.

3. Rule

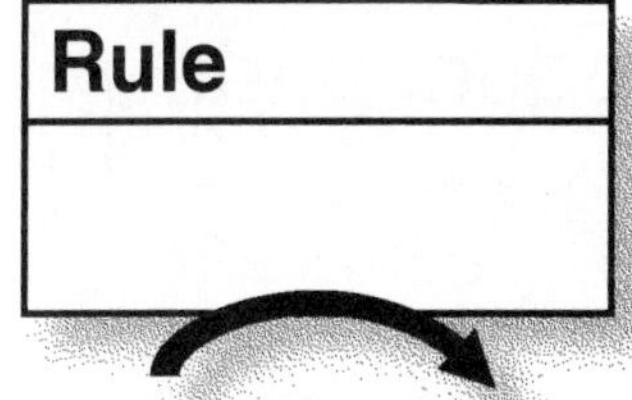

210  200 190

4. Rule

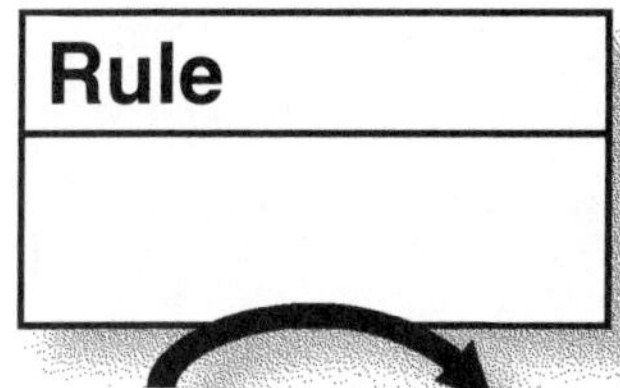

$0.37 $0.47 $0.57  

5. Rule

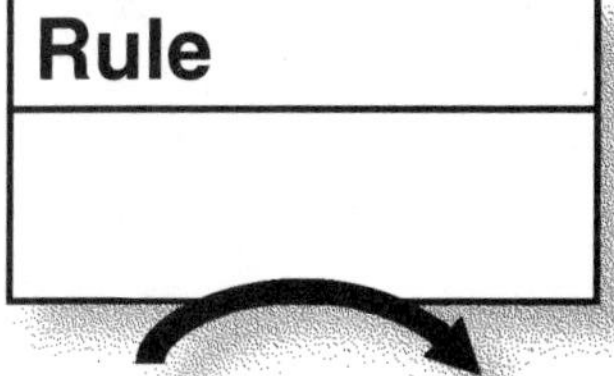

26  30 34

6. Rule

15 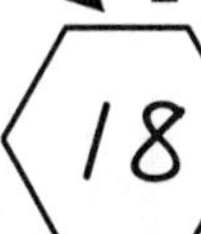 18   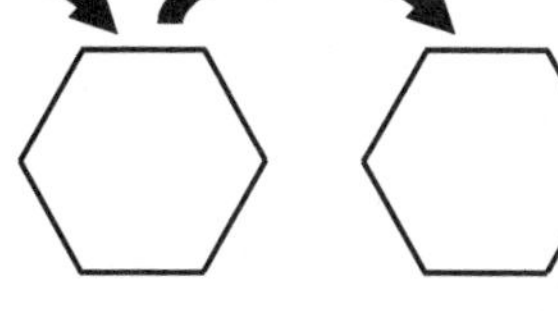

Name Date

Practice Set 72

Write the fraction for the shaded part.

1.

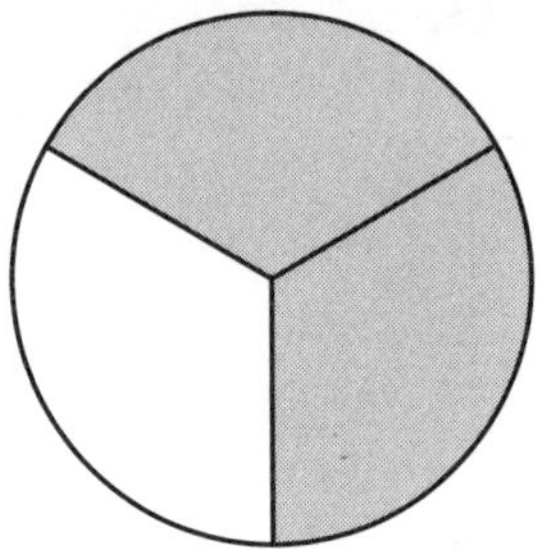

☐ parts that are shaded

☐ number of equal parts

2.

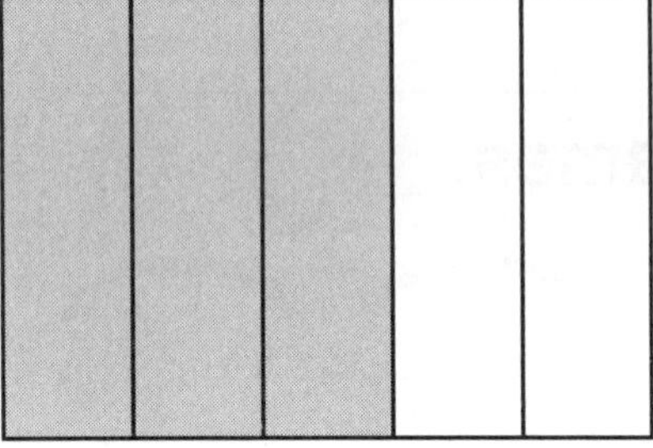

☐ parts that are shaded

☐ number of equal parts

Write 5 more names for the number.

3. **25**

10 + 5 + 5 + 5

30 − 5

4. **40**

38 + 2

50 − 10

Use with or after Lesson 9.7.

Name Date

Practice Set 73

1. Write the fraction.

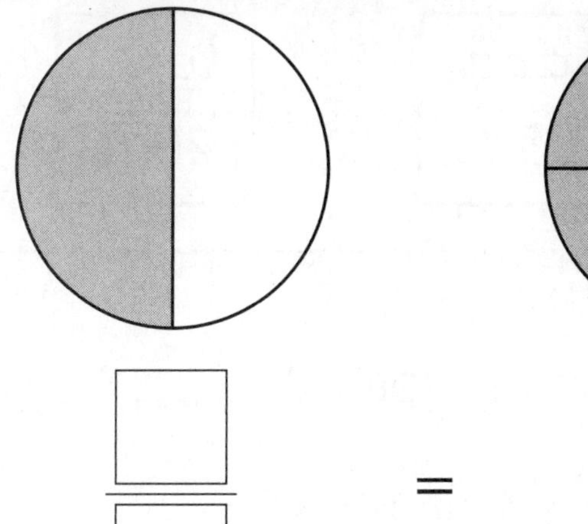

□/□ = □/□

Write the number.

Example four hundred fifteen 415

2. ninety-two ________

3. seven hundred eighty-three ________

4. two hundred seven ________

Use the three digits.
Write the smallest and largest numbers.

Example 2, 8, 5 smallest 258 largest 852

5. 7, 9, 3 smallest ______ largest ______

6. 9, 1, 4 smallest ______ largest ______

7. 6, 8, 5 smallest ______ largest ______

Name Date

Practice Set 74

Animal Weights

fox	goose	dog	koala
14 lb	18 lb	18 lb	20 lb

1. Which weight has the most stick-on notes? ________

2. What is the **typical** weight of the 4 animals?

   ______ pounds

3. What is the **middle** weight of the 4 animals?

   ______ pounds

---

4. Complete the grid.

231	232	233	234	235			238	239	240
241				245		247		249	
		253					258		260
261					266				
271		273	274			277			280
		283					288	289	
									300

Use with or after Lesson 10.1.

Name Date

Practice Set 75

Record the time.

1.

______:______

2.

______:______

Use <, >, or =.

< means *is less than*

> means *is greater than*

= means *is equal to*

3. 2 dimes ☐ 15¢

4. 25¢ ☐ 6 nickels

5. 49¢ ☐ $0.49

6. 13 pennies ☐ 2 nickels

7. 1 quarter, 1 dime, 2 pennies ☐ $0.38

8. 52¢ ☐ 2 quarters, 2 pennies

Name Date

Practice Set 76

Mark the coins you need.

1. 

74¢

2. 

49¢

3. 

85¢

Addition Patterns

4. $4 + 10 =$ ____

5. $4 + 20 =$ ____

6. $4 + 30 =$ ____

7. $4 + 40 =$ ____

8. $4 + 50 =$ ____

Subtraction Patterns

9. ____ $= 62 - 10$

10. ____ $= 62 - 20$

11. ____ $= 62 - 30$

12. ____ $= 62 - 40$

13. ____ $= 62 - 50$

Name Date

Practice Set 77

Solve each problem.

1. Which costs more, the elephant or the dinosaur?

____

How much more? __________¢ more

2. Which costs less, the dinosaur or the plane?

____

How much less? $0.__________ less

3. Which costs more, 2 dinosaurs or a magnet?

____

How much more? __________¢ more

4. If you paid for an elephant with 3 quarters, how much change would you get?

I would get __________¢ change.

Name Date

Practice Set 78

1. Color only the polygons.

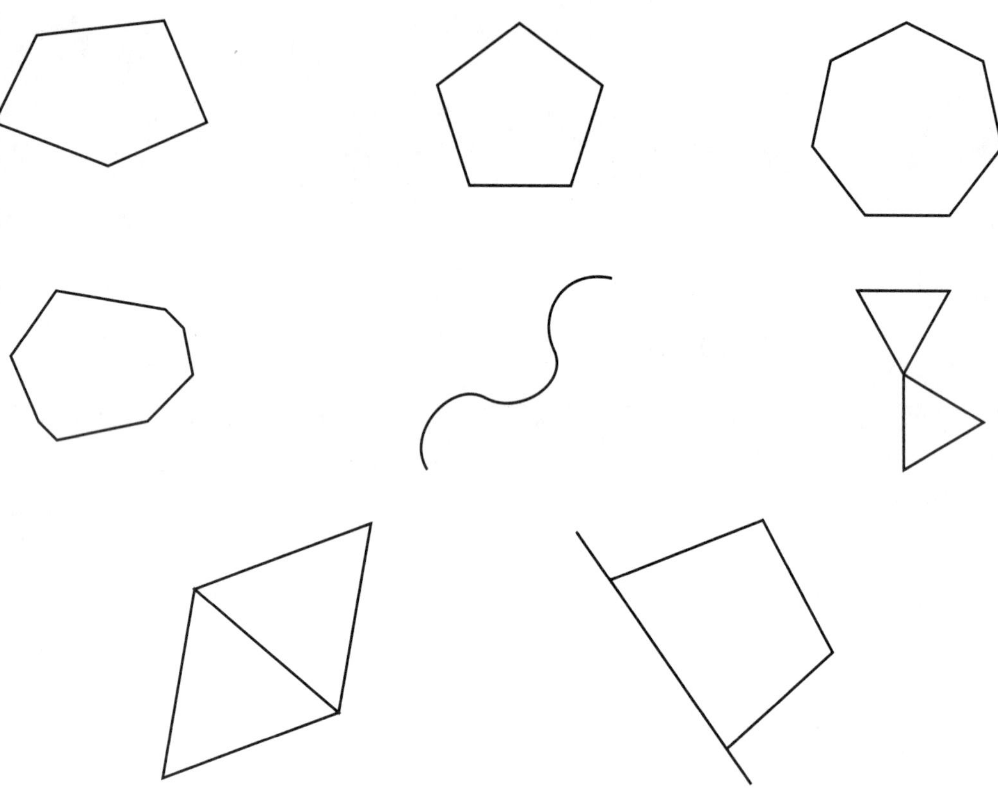

Mark the end of the line segment.

2. 8 centimeters

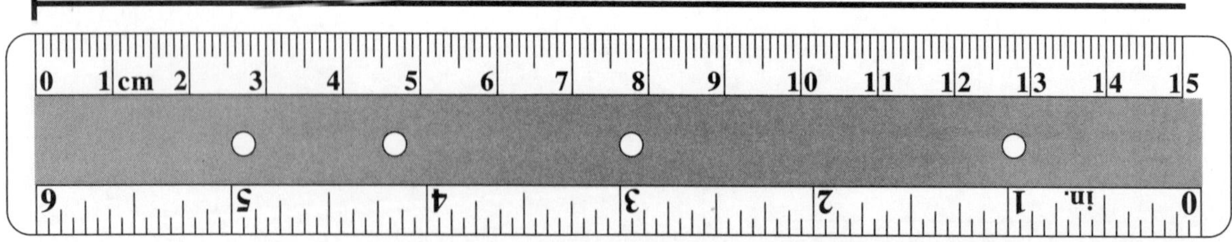

3. 14 centimeters

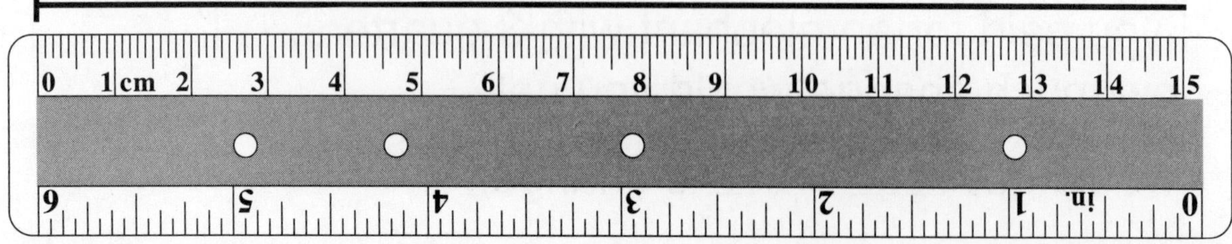

Use with or after Lesson 10.5.

Name Date

Practice Set 79

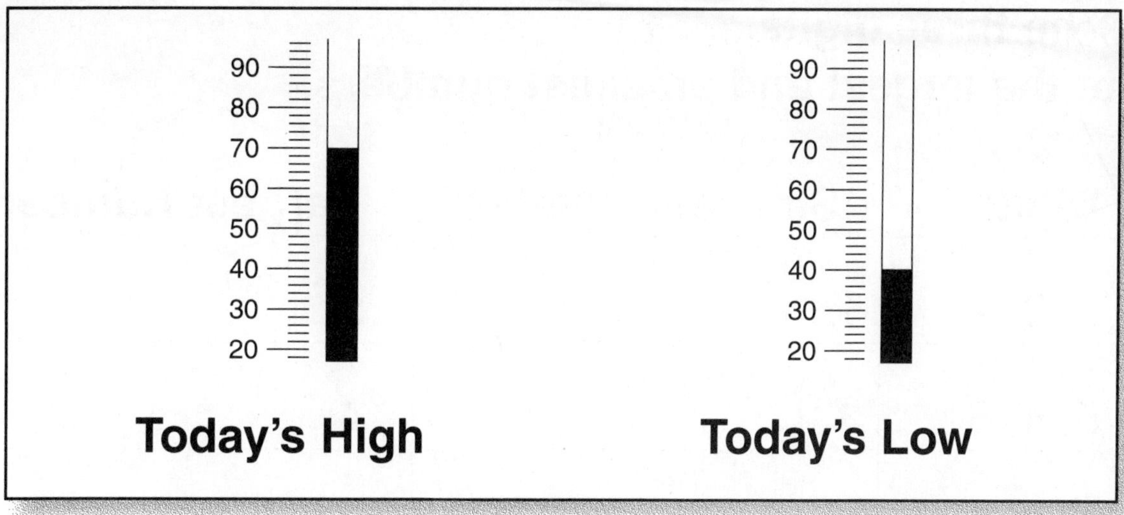

1. What is the difference between the two temperatures?

_____ °F is the difference.

Count by 10s. Fill in the missing numbers.

2. 50, 60, ___, ___, ___, 100, ___, ___, ___

3. 84, 94, ___, ___, 124, ___, ___, ___, ___

4. 127, 137, ___, ___, ___, ___, ___, ___, 207

5. 225, 235, ___, ___, ___, ___, ___, 295, ___

6. Write two **even** numbers between 250 and 300.

_____, _____

7. Write two **odd** numbers between 100 and 150.

_____, _____

Name Date

Practice Set 80

Use the three digits.
Write the largest and smallest numbers.

Digits	Smallest Number	Largest Number
3, 2, 7	**1.**	**2.**
5, 4, 8	**3.**	**4.**
2, 7, 9	**5.**	**6.**
6, 4, 6	**7.**	**8.**
1, 5, 3	**9.**	**10.**

Write the missing numbers in the Fact Triangle.
Then finish the turn-around facts.

11.

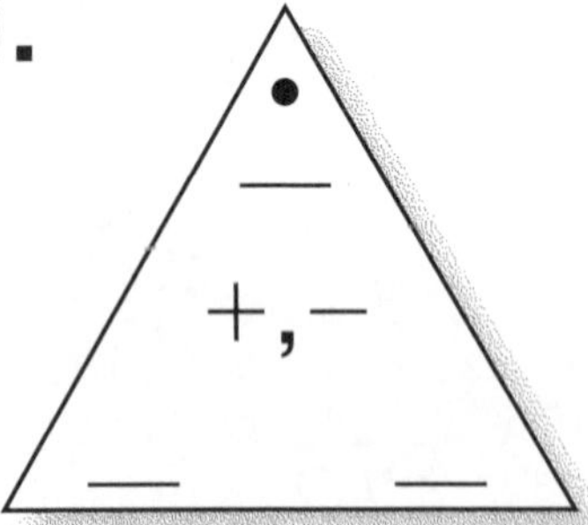

____ + 5 = 7

7 = 5 + ____

12.

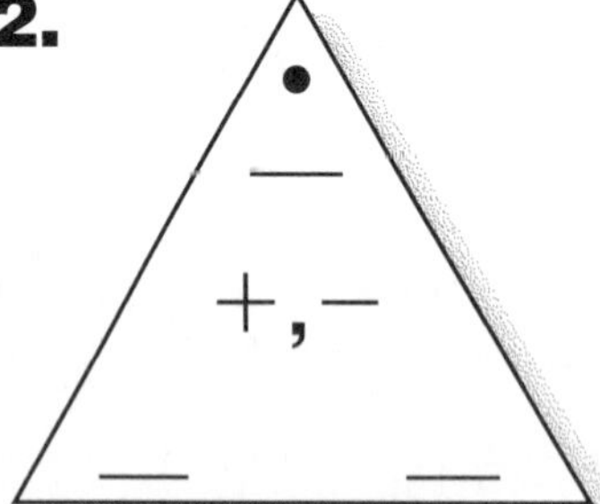

____ = 8 + 3

3 + 8 = ____

13.

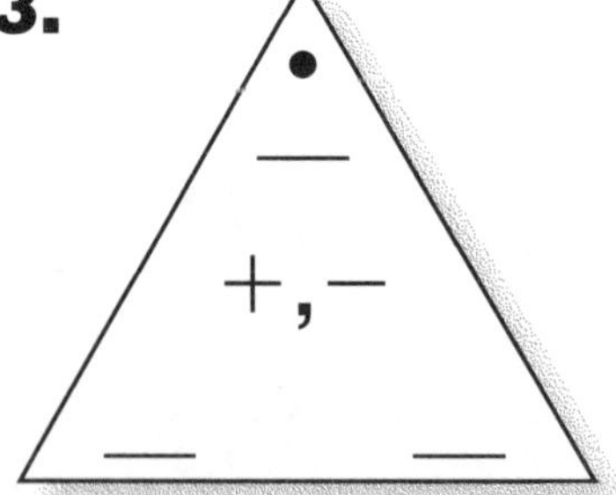

4 + ____ = 10

10 = ____ + 4

Use with or after Lesson 10.7.